# THE NUREMBERG TRIALS

# THE NUREMBERG TRIALS

## THE NAZIS BROUGHT TO JUSTICE

**ALEXANDER MACDONALD**

**Picture Credits**

**Corbis Images:** 18 (Bettmann); 21; 37 (Hulton-Deutsch Collection); 45 (dpa); 67 (Berliner Verlag/Archiv/dpa); 74 (Bettmann); 83 (dpa); 90 (Hulton-Deutsch Collection); 97 (Agentur Voller Ernst/dpa); 100 (Hulton-Deutsch Collection); 106 (Hulton-Deutsch Collection); 126 (Bettmann)

**Getty Images:** 52 (Ullstein Bild); 115 (Imagno); 120 (Apic); 142 (Paul Popper/Popperfoto); 151; 172 (Heinrich Hoffmann/Ullstein Bild)

**Wikimedia Commons:** 6; 13; 23; 32; 57; 88; 110 (both); 129 (both); 135; 154; 155; 159; 165; 179

This edition published in 2022 by Arcturus Publishing Limited
26/27 Bickels Yard, 151–153 Bermondsey Street,
London SE1 3HA

Copyright © Arcturus Holdings Limited

All rights reserved. No part of this publication may be reproduced, stored in a retrieval system, or transmitted, in any form or by any means, electronic, mechanical, photocopying, recording or otherwise, without prior written permission in accordance with the provisions of the Copyright Act 1956 (as amended). Any person or persons who do any unauthorised act in relation to this publication may be liable to criminal prosecution and civil claims for damages.

DA004653UK

Printed in the UK

# Contents

Introduction   6

Chapter One – The Road to Nuremberg   9
Chapter Two – The Accused   17
Chapter Three – The Tribunal   23
Chapter Four – Opening the Prosecution   31
Chapter Five – 'No Mere Willing Tools'   43
Chapter Six – Presenting the Evidence   56
Chapter Seven – War Crimes   64
Chapter Eight – Devastation in the East   73
Chapter Nine – Opening for the Defence   85
Chapter Ten – Hitler's Henchmen   97
Chapter Eleven – Architects of the Holocaust   108
Chapter Twelve – The Money Men   118
Chapter Thirteen – War Horses   125
Chapter Fourteen – Pusillanimous Patriots   135
Chapter Fifteen – Closing Speeches   152
Chapter Sixteen – Illegal Organizations   166
Chapter Seventeen – Final Statements   174
Chapter Eighteen – The Judgement   178

Epilogue   181

Index   184

# Introduction

At exactly 10 am on 20 November 1945, Sir Geoffrey Lawrence banged his gavel on the desk in the Palace of Justice in Nuremberg. As presiding judge, he made an opening statement, saying: 'The trial which is now about to begin is unique in the history of the jurisprudence of the world.'

*The eyes of the world were on the Palace of Justice in November 1945 when US Supreme Court judge Robert H. Jackson opened the case for the prosecution.*

# INTRODUCTION

This was the first time that those defeated in a war had been put on trial by an international court of the victors. The proceedings were taking place under the auspices of the United Kingdom, the United States, the Republic of France and the Union of Soviet Socialist Republics.

The reason these nations took this step became clear on the second day of the trial when US Supreme Court judge Robert H. Jackson made the opening statement for the prosecution.

'The wrongs which we seek to condemn and punish have been so calculated, so malignant, and so devastating, that civilization cannot tolerate their being ignored, because it cannot survive their being repeated,' he said. 'That four great nations, flushed with victory and stung with injury stay the hand of vengeance and voluntarily submit their captive enemies to the judgment of the law is one of the most significant tributes that Power has ever paid to Reason.'

He conceded that the tribunal was both novel and experimental, but the four nations conducting it had the support of another 17 in their effort 'to utilize international law to meet the greatest menace of our times – aggressive war'.

Surveying the defendants, Jackson said: 'In the prisoners' dock sit twenty-odd broken men. Reproached by the humiliation of those they have led almost as bitterly as by the desolation of those they have attacked, their personal capacity for evil is forever past. It is hard now to perceive in these men as captives the power by which as Nazi leaders they once dominated much of the world and terrified most of it. Merely as individuals their fate is of little consequence to the world.

'What makes this inquest significant is that these prisoners represent sinister influences that will lurk in the world long after their bodies have returned to dust. We will show them to be living symbols of racial hatreds, of terrorism and violence, and of the arrogance and cruelty of power. They are symbols of fierce nationalisms and of militarism, of intrigue and war-making which have embroiled Europe generation after generation, crushing its manhood, destroying its homes, and impoverishing its life. They have so identified themselves with the philosophies they conceived and with the forces they directed that any tenderness to them is a victory and an encouragement to all the evils which are attached to their names.'

These 21 Nazi leaders were charged with crimes against peace, war crimes, and crimes against humanity – and with having a common plan or conspiracy to commit those crimes. (In total 24 Nazis were indicted at Nuremberg but only 21 faced trial, because one was considered too ill and senile, one was missing and one committed suicide in custody.)

This was the first of 12 trials, involving more than a hundred defendants and several different courts, that took place at Nuremberg from 1945 to 1949. The trial of 16 German judges and officials of the justice ministry broke new ground, considering the criminal responsibility of judges who enforce immoral laws. Doctors were tried for the hideous experiments they conducted on inmates of concentration camps and members of Einsatzgruppen – death squads – were tried for the indiscriminate murder of civilians.

While the Nuremberg Trials had no precedent, they set one. The following year, 1946, Japanese war leaders were put on trial in Tokyo. The principles established at Nuremberg were written into international conventions. International criminal tribunals have been set up to try war criminals from Rwanda and the former Yugoslavia and the International Criminal Court began sitting in The Hague in the Netherlands in 2002.

## Chapter One
# The Road to Nuremberg

Normally in war, defeat was punishment enough. The losers in war were either killed on the battlefield or found themselves in the hands of the victors, who could do what they liked with them. Until modern times, there was no clear definition of what constituted a war crime and, largely, the victors found it expedient to be magnanimous.

However, after the wholesale slaughter of the First World War, the victorious allies sought to bring enemy war criminals to book. In the Versailles Treaty that concluded the war, Kaiser Wilhelm II was publicly arraigned for 'a supreme offence against international morality and the sanctity of treaties'. He was to be brought before a special tribunal composed of five judges from the US, the UK, France, Italy and Japan.

Others who had violated the laws and customs of war were also to be brought before tribunals and punished, and the German government was to be obliged to hand them over, along with any evidence that might help convict them.

When the treaty was signed on 28 June 1919, a note was sent to the Dutch government, requesting the extradition of the former kaiser, who had been granted asylum in the Netherlands after abdicating in November 1918. However, the Dutch refused to comply, maintaining that to do so would violate Dutch neutrality.

In February 1920, the Allies submitted a list of 900 names to the German government, including that of the chief of the general staff, Field Marshal Paul von Hindenburg, who went on to become the president of Germany who made Adolf Hitler chancellor. It, too, refused to hand over those named, but asked instead to be allowed to try them in German courts. The Allies agreed. The list was then whittled down to 45, of whom only 12 came to court.

The trial took place before the Reichsgericht – or Supreme Court – in Leipzig, comprising seven judges. Just six of those named were convicted and sentenced to between six months and four years imprisonment. The highest-ranking was a captain. The Allies thought that the big fish had got off the hook, while those who had been prosecuted had been given a mere slap on the wrist. However, Germany felt it was unfair that only Germans were prosecuted when atrocities had been committed on both sides. The trials also seemed to flout established legal principles, causing great resentment in Germany, especially among former servicemen. They petered out in November 1922. Outrage at the humiliation inflicted by these trials fuelled Hitler's 'Beer Hall Putsch' – a failed Nazi attempt at a coup – in 1923.

Meanwhile the whole German nation was being punished by the 'war guilt' clause in the Versailles Treaty and the huge reparations they were being forced to pay. These grievances contributed to the rise of Nazism, resulting in the Second World War. Those gathered at Nuremberg had decided that this must not be allowed to happen again.

### *War like no other*

It was plain to those who lived through it that the Second World War was like no other war. Not only had more than 50 million people died during the fighting and millions more been wounded, some permanently disabled, but also countless homes had been destroyed and lives wrecked. This war had been waged in the service of an ideology that demanded the dispossession, subjugation and elimination of millions of innocent people. Death squads following the advancing German troops had ruthlessly murdered civilians. Millions more had been used as forced labour and herded into concentration camps and death camps. Indeed, that indictment of the 24 Nazi leaders at Nuremberg brought a new word into the English language – genocide. Count 3 stated that the defendants 'conducted deliberate and systematic genocide – namely, the extermination of racial and national groups ....' Clearly, such crimes could not go unpunished.

Hitler had made no secret of his intentions. He had written of his desire to rid Germany of its Jewish population and subjugate the Slav people to the east, whom he considered subhuman. As early as April 1940, the British and French governments, and the Polish government-in-exile, issued 'a formal and public protest to the conscience of the world against the action of the German government whom they must hold responsible for these crimes which cannot remain unpunished'.

Even before the United States entered the war, President Franklin D. Roosevelt warned Germany that 'one day a frightful retribution' would be exacted for the summary execution of hostages in France. The British prime minister Winston Churchill concurred. In November 1941, he said: 'The massacres of the French are an example of what Hitler's Nazis are doing in many other countries under their yoke. The atrocities committed in Poland, Yugoslavia, Norway, Holland, Belgium, and particularly behind the German front in Russia, exceeds anything that has been known since the darkest and most bestial ages of humanity. The punishment of these crimes should now be counted among the major goals of the war.'

Representatives of nine occupied countries in Europe met

## CHAPTER ONE

in the Palace of St James in London and declared 'among their principal war aims the punishment, through the channel of organized justice, of those guilty of or responsible for these crimes, whether they have ordered them, perpetrated them or participated in them'.

In July 1942, Churchill was contemplating what would happen if Hitler fell into British hands. 'We shall certainly put him to death,' he said. 'Instrument – electric chair, for gangsters, no doubt available on lend-lease.'

By July the following year, he had decided that other Nazi leaders should be summarily shot rather than put on trial. He suggested that a list of 50 or so be drawn up. When any were caught by advancing troops, they could be executed on the spot without reference to higher authority. This could be made legal if Parliament passed an act of attainder, outlawing then. However, acts of attainder are specifically banned by the US Constitution.

Following the Red Army's victory in the Battle of Stalingrad, turning the tide on the Eastern Front, the Soviet premier Joseph Stalin signed the 'Statement on Atrocities', largely written by Churchill, which was part of the Moscow Declarations in October 1943. It said that German soldiers and members of the Nazi Party who had taken part in atrocities, massacres and executions would be sent back to the countries in which these abominable deeds had been done, for punishment, and 'German criminals whose offences have no particular geographical location ... will be punished by joint decision of the governments of the Allies'.

The United Nations War Crimes Commission was set up in London to collect information on war crimes. But it had no Russian representative, as Stalin had insisted that each of the Soviet republics be represented separately, which would have proved too unwieldly.

# The Road to Nuremberg

## Tehran Conference

When Churchill, Stalin and Roosevelt met in Tehran in November 1943, Stalin proposed executing 50,000–100,000 German staff officers. Churchill, who had served as an officer himself, was against the idea of executing soldiers who had fought for their country and said he would rather be 'taken out into the courtyard and shot' himself than sanction such a thing. Aiming to lower the temperature, Roosevelt said that maybe 49,000 would do.

*At a meeting in Tehran in November 1943, Stalin, Roosevelt and Churchill began to discuss what to do with Nazi war criminals once the war was won.*

Still, when it came to killing committed Nazis Churchill was not so pernickety and the British Ambassador in Moscow reassured the Russians on this point, saying: 'I am sure that the political decision that Mr Churchill

# CHAPTER ONE

has in mind will be accompanied by all the necessary formalities.'

Stalin was all for show trials, having used them to purge opposition in the Soviet Union in the 1930s. But Churchill and Roosevelt were frightened that putting Hitler and his henchmen on trial would give them a forum in which they could justify their actions. The massacre of 84 US prisoners of war by Schutzstaffel (SS) troops at Malmedy, Belgium, during the Battle of the Bulge in December 1944 strengthened America's thirst for vengeance.

The summary execution of major war criminals was advocated by the US secretary of the treasury, Henry Morgenthau, who had the ear of the president. However, the secretary of war, Henry Stimson, argued that establishing the guilt of the Nazi regime before an international tribunal would play a vital part in rehabilitating the German people who had, after all, voted Hitler into power in the first place. What was needed was some legal and practical way of going about it.

Stimson assigned Lieutenant Colonel Murray Bernays, an attorney at the War Department, to the task. The US Constitution prohibited *ex post facto* laws – that is, laws made up after the event to criminalize actions that were not illegal when they were committed. Neither was it practical to try separately everyone who committed a crime during the war. Nor was it right to punish the entire German people for something their leaders had done.

Bernays suggested that the laws of criminal conspiracy could be used. The allegation would be that the Third Reich was a premeditated criminal enterprise. Consequently members of the Nazi government, the Nazi Party, certain state agencies, the Sturmabteilung (SA) paramilitaries, the SS elite troops and the Gestapo secret police could be convicted and condemned simply on the basis of their membership. The leaders could not claim that they were not responsible for atrocities because they did not personally take part in them.

Roosevelt continued to sit on the fence. But when he died on 12 April 1945, his successor, President Harry S. Truman, was won over. He appointed Supreme Court justice Robert H. Jackson 'chief of counsel for the prosecution of Axis criminals' – that is, war criminals from Germany, Italy, Japan and their allies. And, eventually, the British were persuaded that execution without trial was contrary to the principles of common law.

### *The London Charter*
After appalling images of the Holocaust had filled the newsreels, there was an increasing appetite for those responsible to be brought to justice. Lawyers from the four major powers – the US, UK, USSR and France – met in London in July to discuss the details of the trial.

They came up with the three categories of crime – crimes against peace, war crimes and crimes against humanity. When it was pointed out that formulating these new offences risked creating *ex post facto* laws, Jackson said: 'Aren't murder, torture and enslavement crimes recognized by all civilized people?'

Another potential pitfall was that after Nazi Germany had invaded the west of Poland on 1 September 1939, starting the Second World War, the Soviet Union had occupied the east of the country on 17 September. To avoid the defence of *tu quoque* – 'you also' – the Soviets decided that attack was the best form of defence and insisted on adding to the indictment the massacre of a thousand Polish officers in the Katyn Forest, which they themselves had been responsible for.

There was also a problem with procedure. The British

## CHAPTER ONE

and Americans had an adversarial system that was very different from the French and Soviet systems in which witnesses were examined by a panel of investigating judges. So a hybrid was devised. There would be opposing lawyers for the prosecution and the defence, as in the Anglo-Saxon system, but there would be no jury; judgment would be passed by a panel of four judges, one from each of the four powers, with four alternates in reserve should any of them fall ill.

These principles were embodied in the London Charter of the International Military Tribunal, which was signed on 8 August 1945.

### The venue

Next a venue had to be decided on. The Soviets favoured Berlin, but this was impractical because the city had been devastated by Allied bombing. The Palace of Justice in Nuremberg incorporated a large prison, about 80 courtrooms and some 530 offices – and was largely undamaged. The Nazi Party had held its rallies in the city and the anti-Semitic laws that among other things stripped Jews of their German citizenship had been introduced at a rally there in 1935 and were known at the Nuremberg Laws. It seemed fitting that the Nazi Party and its cohorts should meet their demise there.

A compromise was reached. According to the London Charter, Berlin was to be the permanent home of the International Military Tribunal; the first formal session took place there under Soviet Major-General Iona Timofeevich Nikitchenko on 18 October 1945. But the first trial was to take place in Nuremberg, starting on 20 November 1945.

## Chapter Two
# The Accused

The worst of the Nazis – Adolf Hitler; head of the SS and principle architect of the Holocaust Heinrich Himmler; and propaganda minister Joseph Goebbels – had committed suicide. Others, such as Adolf Eichmann, the bureaucrat who organized the Holocaust, and Josef Mengele, the doctor who performed hideous experiments on the inmates of Auschwitz, had eluded capture. However, 24 top Nazis were indicted, along with seven organizations.

The highest-ranking was Reichsmarschall Hermann Göring. He had joined the Nazi Party in 1922 and had risen to become its second-highest-ranking member. When Hitler seized power, he established the Gestapo, the secret political police. As head of the Luftwaffe – the German Air Force – he became Hitler's designated successor in 1941. In April 1945, believing Hitler to be hopelessly surrounded in Berlin, he assumed command, only to be repudiated by the Führer. He surrendered to the Americans with his wife, daughter, valet and 16 pieces of matching luggage – along with 20,000 of the paracodeine tablets to which he was addicted – evidently expecting to be treated as a plenipotentiary.

Indeed, he was initially wined and dined by the American Seventh Army who had captured him. He was photographed with a glass of champagne in hand alongside the flag of the Texas division to whom he had surrendered. When this got bad press, he was taken to a prisoner of war camp at Augsburg, then to Camp Ashcan – formerly the Palace

## CHAPTER TWO

*Once Hitler's deputy, Herman Göring assumed that he would be treated as an honoured adversary by the Allies, not a common criminal.*

Hotel – in Mondorf-les-Bains, near Luxembourg, where senior Nazis were interrogated.

## The Accused

### In the dock

Beside Göring in the dock would be Rudolf Hess, who had been Hitler's deputy until he had secretly flown to Britain in 1941 in what seems to have been an attempt to broker a peace deal. He complained of amnesia and appeared distracted, but medical personnel who examined Hess reported he was not insane and was fit to stand trial.

Also on trial was Admiral Karl Dönitz, who was president of what was left of Germany for just a few days after Hitler's suicide. As leader of the Kriegsmarine, he instigated the U-boat campaign against the merchant shipping that brought supplies from the United States and Canada to Britain.

Hans Frank had been minister of justice and governor-general of occupied Poland. Wilhelm Frick was the author of the anti-Semitic Nuremberg Laws. Propagandist Julius Streicher had been the editor of the anti-Semitic weekly newspaper *Der Stürmer* ('The Attacker'). Alfred Rosenberg was the Nazi ideologist who promoted racial theory and the persecution of the Jews, later becoming Reichminister for the occupied eastern territories.

Ernst Kaltenbrunner had been the leader of the Austrian SS and Germany's Reich Security Main Office (RSHA), which administered the Holocaust. Foreign minister Joachim von Ribbentrop negotiated the German-Soviet Non-aggression Pact – also known as the Molotov-Ribbentrop Pact – in August 1939; this allowed Hitler, then Stalin, to invade Poland. Ribbentrop also signed the Tripartite Pact with allies Italy and Japan in 1940, before the German-Soviet Pact was abrogated by the Nazis' attack on the USSR the following year. Ribbentrop's predecessor Konstantin von Neurath was also on trial. As Reichsprotektor for Bohemia and Moravia, he had imposed the Nuremberg Laws there.

Fritz Sauckel was responsible for slave labour, overseeing

the deportation of some 5 million people. Alfred Jodl was the German general in charge of most of Hitler's military campaigns, while Field Marshal Wilhelm Keitel was head of the German high command. Erich Raeder was Commander-in-Chief of the German Navy.

Austrian Nazi leader Arthur Seyss-Inquart was chancellor of Austria during the Anschluss – the annexation of Austria by Germany in 1938. After serving as governor of the new province of Austria, he was deputy governor of Poland, before becoming Reichskommissar of the occupied Netherlands.

Economist Walther Funk was the Third Reich's minister of economic affairs and president of the Reichsbank. His predecessor in the economics ministry, Hjalmar Schacht, was also on trial. Baldur von Schirach was head of the Hitler Youth. Albert Speer was minister for armaments and war production, which used slave labour.

Franz von Papen had stepped down as German chancellor to make way for Hitler and served, briefly, as his vice chancellor. And Hans Fritzsche had worked under Goebbels at the propaganda ministry.

## *In absentia*

Head of the party chancellery and Hitler's right-hand man Martin Bormann had disappeared on 1 May 1945 and was tried *in absentia*. Head of German labour Robert Ley had been indicted, but committed suicide in prison, hanging himself with a towel in the lavatory, while awaiting trial. The industrialist Gustav Krupp von Bohlen und Halbach, who had helped finance Hitler's rise to power and profited from armament production, was found to be too ill and senile to stand trial.

Seven organizations were also on trial: the leadership corps of the Nazi Party; the Reich cabinet; the elite black-shirted Schutzstaffel (SS); their intelligence service the

# The Accused

*Hitler's trusted lieutenant Martin Bormann disappeared from the Führer's bunker in April 1945 and was tried in absentia at Nuremberg.*

## CHAPTER TWO

Sicherheitsdienst (SD); the Gestapo secret police; the brown-shirted Sturmabteilung (SA); and the general staff and high command of the German armed forces.

### Security

The defendants were kept in separate cells with a guard stationed outside each day and night. They were not allowed to talk to each other during their 20-minute exercise period or in the showers. They were brought up to the courtroom one by one in an elevator and passed through a series of checkpoints, each telephoning ahead on the prisoner's arrival. The war in Europe had been over barely six months and security was tight. There was a fear that a 'Werewolf' organization of dedicated Nazis was still operating.

In the dock, they sat on two wooden benches with a line of white-helmeted US military policemen behind them. The policemen wore a special insignia designed by Colonel Burton C. Andrus, commandant of the prison there, and white truncheons that were sawn-off mop handles. Andrus lectured the defendants beforehand, warning them to co-operate. Any attempt to disrupt the proceedings would be met with punishment.

Defendants still on speaking terms were permitted to exchange opinions in the dock, during recesses. They were not allowed to wear any military insignia, nor could military men be addressed by rank – otherwise they would have had to be treated in accordance with the Geneva Convention, which prohibits solitary confinement.

As some of the defendants had been arrested in only the clothes they stood up in, a Nuremberg tailor was employed to run up suits for them. (According to the *New York Times* Frank had been captured wearing 'only lace panties'.) Court suits could only be worn during court appearances and had to be taken off directly the prisoner returned to his cell.

## Chapter Three
# The Tribunal

The president of the tribunal was British – Colonel Sir Geoffrey Lawrence, who had fought in France during the First World War, then risen to become Attorney-General and Lord Justice of Appeal. In private, he was a collector of china and breeder of Guernsey cows, whose pedigrees he knew by heart. And as counsel to the Jockey Club, he was also a devotee of the turf. One American lawyer said: ''ollywood would have cast him. He was like God.'

Fritzsche, who was short, said Lawrence was 'like a giant'. And once, when Lawrence put a stop to a courtroom

*The Soviet and British judges, left to right: Lieutenant-Colonel A.F. Volchkov, Major-General I.T. Nikitchenko, Sir Norman Birkett, Sir Geoffrey Lawrence and Judge Francis B. Biddle.*

## CHAPTER THREE

dispute, Göring said: 'Do you hear the wings of the Angel of Death?'

After the opening session, someone stole Lawrence's oak gavel, leaving him to tap a pen or pencil on the bench whenever he needed to restore order. This did nothing to lessen his authority. The alternate British judge was Sir Norman Birkett, who sat in the High Court. He had a formidable mind, kept a detailed account of the proceedings and wrote the judgments.

The American judge was Francis B. Biddle, a former attorney-general who had served in the US Army in 1918 and was another fierce intellect. His alternate was John J. Parker, who had been nominated for the Supreme Court but been rejected by one vote.

The French put up Henri Donnedieu de Vabres, professor of criminal law at Paris University. His alternate was Robert Falco, who had won the *Légion d'honneur* during the Franco-Prussian War of 1870–1. He had been dismissed from his post on the Paris Court of Appeal in 1944 because of his Jewish ancestry.

The lead Soviet judge was Major-General I.T. Nikitchenko, who fought in the Russian Civil War of 1918–21 and had presided over show trials during Stalin's Great Purges of 1936–8. The outcome of the trials was clear to him from the outset: 'We are dealing here with the chief war criminals who have already been convicted and whose conviction has been already announced by both the Moscow and Crimea [Yalta] declarations by the heads of the [Allied] governments,' he said. 'The whole idea is to secure quick and just punishment for the crime.'

His alternate was Lieutenant-Colonel Alexander Fedorovich Volchkov, who had worked in the film industry before entering the law.

As president of the court, Lawrence sat just right of the

centre, with Birkett to his right, followed by Nikitchenko and Volchkov. To the left of centre, came Biddle, then Parker, followed by de Vabres and Falco. This placed the four English-speaking judges together. The wily Biddle, who arranged the seating, gave himself equal prominence with Lawrence as he could speak fluent French.

All the judges wore judicial robes, with the exception of the Soviets who wore military uniforms. Behind each pair was their national flag.

## *The prosecutors*

The British prosecutor was Attorney-General Hartley Shawcross, who had already prosecuted the treason trials of William Joyce, the propagandist 'Lord Haw-Haw', and John Amery, son of a cabinet minister in Churchill's government who started the British Free Corps in Germany. They were to hang. Busy with other things, Shawcross provided only the opening and closing statements, while the rest of the British case was presented by his deputy, Solicitor-General Sir David Maxwell Fyfe.

The US prosecution team was led by Robert H. Jackson, a former US solicitor-general and US attorney-general, as well as a Supreme Court judge. He described his work at Nuremberg as 'infinitely more important than my work on the Supreme Court'.

The French sent former French Resistance leader and winner of the Légion d'Honneur and the Croix de Guerre François de Menthon. He was the attorney-general of France who also oversaw the trial of Marshal Philippe Pétain and members of his collaborationist Vichy government. In his opening speech, de Menthon defined a crime against humanity as 'crime against human laws, motivated by an ideology that is a crime against the spirit, returning humanity to barbarism'. He resigned in January 1946 to take up active politics and was replaced by Auguste Champetier de Ribes, another former French Resistance leader.

The Soviet Union put up Lieutenant-General Roman Andreyovich Rudenko, then the chief prosecutor of the Ukraine and commandant of NKVD Special Camp Nr 7. This was the former Nazi concentration camp of Sachsenhausen where, under Soviet control, more than 12,000 died of malnutrition and disease.

## Counsel for the defence

After the defendants were served with their indictments on 19 October, they were told to find themselves lawyers. Acknowledging this, Keitel tried to click his heels, but the effect was rather spoilt by the felt slippers the prisoners were forced to wear. Frank burst into tears at the prospect of a trial. Ribbentrop and Rosenberg trembled. No fewer than nine of the defendants asked for the same Munich lawyer, Gustav von Scanzoni, but he had emigrated to Switzerland and turned them all down.

Göring was scornful of the very idea of finding German lawyers to defend them. He compiled a list of eight who either turned him down flat or could not be located. He then asked assistant prosecutor Maxwell Fyfe to help him draw up a list of witnesses and prepare his case. This was an unusual step in Anglo-Saxon jurisprudence, but not so unusual under the Continental European system. Maxwell Fyfe suggested Otto Stahmer, a high court judge from Kiel with a good reputation, though he had little or no criminal experience. Stahmer was delighted with the appointment, saying that he was 'not finding it difficult to persuade himself of Göring's innocence'. It would prove more difficult to persuade others, though.

The Krupp family had asked Andrew Clark, KC, a

barrister at the Chancery, to represent their patriarch in the preliminary hearings. But the General Council of the Bar said that it was 'undesirable that a member of the English Bar should appear for the defence' – even though Major T.C.M. Winwood had acted as counsel for the defence for camp commandant Josef Kramer and three others at the earlier Belsen trial. The Krupps had to look elsewhere.

Von Papen was represented by Dr Egon Kubuschok, who was also defending the Reich cabinet. Papen praised his 'keen intelligence', while Norman Birkett said of Kubuschok: 'He is not exactly to be described as a windbag, because that implies some powers of rhetoric and possible eloquence – of these qualities this man is strikingly bereft.'

Rosenberg wanted co-defendant Frank, the former minister of justice, to represent him. But the judges thought it was inappropriate to see one of the accused commuting from the dock to the counsel's lectern, then to the witness stand. Nor were they prepared to pay him. Schacht's attorney, Rudolf Dix, returned to Berlin after the retainer of 10,000 marks he requested was not forthcoming. Eventually the judges agreed to give counsels an advance of 4,000 marks, and pay them 2,500 marks a month. This was academic as the only viable currency in Germany at the time was American cigarettes.

Dönitz wanted naval judge Flottenrichter Otto Kranzbühler to defend him. 'If he cannot be reached I have requested that a British or American submarine admiral come here to defend me,' Dönitz said. 'He can understand me. He did the same job.'

### Public attacks

As the trial approached, Biddle fretted that the other defendants would not find lawyers to represent them. He got the court to chastise the occupation authorities for permitting

## CHAPTER THREE

press and other public attacks on the counsels, putting them under the protection of the tribunal.

Former prisoner of war Major Airey Neave, who read the indictments to the accused, circulated a list of 60 lawyers. Hess told him that he did not care who defended him, or whether he was defended at all. The tribunal had to appoint counsel for him. Neave's suggestion that lawyers should be compelled to appear was rejected. Meanwhile some of the defendants asked that Jewish lawyers should not be appointed to appear for them. However distasteful this was to the judges, they felt compelled to comply.

As it was, 18 of the 48 defence lawyers who participated had been members of the Nazi Party. Biddle was happy with this. Why not have Nazis defending the Nazi regime? he argued.

There were safeguards, though. Under the London Charter, the defence had to provide a list of the witnesses they proposed to call for prior approval. In this way judges hoped they could prevent the proceedings becoming a forum for Nazi propaganda.

### Simultaneous translation

While simultaneous translation is now commonplace in the United Nations (UN) and European parliament, the system at Nuremberg was still an experiment. At the UN's precursor, the League of Nations, which had begun in 1931, speeches had to be submitted in advance, then translated and read by interpreters while the speaker delivered the address in their native language.

The IBM system installed in the Palace of Justice had five channels. Channel one carried the verbatim transmission; two carried the English translation; three, Russian; four, French; five, German. The translations were provided by interpreters who were sitting in glass booths to the side of the dock; cables snaked across the floor.

Every participant in the trial had a set of headphones and there were six microphones in the courtroom – one in front of each of the four judges, one in the witness box and one on the lawyer's podium. A yellow light beside the microphone warned the speaker when they were going too fast, while a red one indicated they should stop and repeat what they had just said. Two additional translators sat behind the judges, one between the British and Soviet justices, and one between the American and French, so that they could confer. Usually they had little to do and one was dismissed for snoring.

### *The press*
No fewer than 250 journalists from 23 countries attended the trial. These included novelists John Dos Passos, reporting for *Life* magazine, and Rebecca West, for the *New Yorker*. Some 85 were from the United States, 50 from Britain, 40 from France, five from the Soviet Union, ten from Scandinavia, ten from South and Central America, five from Belgium, three from Switzerland and the remainder from Germany. They sat behind the five counsels' tables – one for each of the participating nations, plus one for the tribunal's secretary.

The room itself was shaped like an amphitheatre, slightly raised on all four sides, with steps leading down to the pit in the centre. In the middle, opposite the witness box, was the lectern used by the prosecuting and defence counsels to conduct cross-examinations or to address the court. Facing it were also a score of court reporters and stenographers, recording the proceedings in shorthand.

There was a movie screen so that newsreel and other footage could be introduced in evidence. Otherwise the walls were panelled in dark oak, with ornate carvings around the doors. Dark green curtains hung over the windows, but a

## CHAPTER THREE

flash of colour was provided by the two dozen defence attorneys, who wore robes of red, purple and black, according to the school they had graduated from.

The courtroom was brightly lit with garish fluorescent lights so the proceedings could be filmed by the cameras that whirred behind a soundproofed screen.

### Checkpoints

Outside, the palace was ringed with checkpoints and gun emplacements after a young woman working in the court library reported a rumour that a group of Bavarian Nazis intended to free the defendants. She happened to be the niece of Field Marshal Erwin Rommel, who been forced by Hitler to commit suicide the previous year.

There were other dangers. Earlier, a roof had to be built over the walkway from the prison to the Palace of Justice after an SS dagger had fallen mysteriously from above and embedded itself in the ground at the feet of Göring, whom Hitler, in his last hours, had denounced as a traitor.

## Chapter Four
## Opening the Prosecution

The French and Soviet delegations tried to delay the opening of the trial because they were not ready. Rudenko was even reported to have been struck down by malaria, but he made a miraculous recovery when the British and Americans, who wanted to get on with it, threatened to publicize their delaying tactics.

The defence counsels then tried to wreck the trial completely when they jointly filed a motion contesting that war had not been outlawed by any recognized international law. This was rejected under Article Three of the London Charter, which said: 'Neither the tribunal, its members nor their alternates can be challenged by the prosecution, or by the defendants or their counsel.'

At 9.30 am on 20 November 1945, the doors of the courtroom were opened. The defendants were already in place behind a low wooden partition. In the front row were Göring in one of his powder-blue uniforms, Hess, Ribbentrop, Keitel, Rosenberg, Frank, Frick, Streicher, Funk and Schacht. Kaltenbrunner would join them later as, at the time, he was suffering from the first of two subarachnoid haemorrhages. He subsequently recovered and although his lawyer attempted to have him excused from the trial on health grounds, the tribunal refused and Kaltenbrunner was forced to attend. The second row was made up of Dönitz, Raeder, von Papen, Seyss-Inquart, Speer, von Neurath and Fritzsche.

## CHAPTER FOUR

*The defendants were not allowed to wear military insignia, otherwise they would have had to have been treated in accordance with the Geneva Conventions.*

At 10 am the marshal announced the imminent entry of the members of the tribunal. The judges filed in. The marshal called the court to order and the room fell silent. Lord Justice Lawrence read a brief statement. Then the indictments were read.

This was a mere formality for the defendants as they had had the indictments read to them before and had received copies of them to study. Göring sat through this with an air of studied indifference. Ribbentrop sweated profusely and Funk sobbed. CBS correspondent William Shirer noted: 'Shorn of the power and the glory and the glittering trappings of Nazidom, how little and mean and mediocre they looked.'

Justices Lawrence and Parker also mopped their brows

**Opening the Prosecution**

under the high-powered lights installed for the movie cameras. Some of the accused fell asleep – they had been awoken at 6 am. Many of the journalists found the courtroom stifling and left, even though the regulations of the court required them to stay in their seats. The following day, the regulations were revised so that they could come and go as they pleased.

## *Pleas*

The following morning, the defendants were asked to enter a plea. Göring, who was called first, tried to read a prepared statement. Lawrence cut him off immediately, saying he must only plead guilty or not guilty.

'I declare myself in the sense of the indictment not guilty,' he said.

His statement was quickly released to the press. In it, he said: 'As Reichsmarschall of the Greater German Reich I accept the political responsibility for all my own acts or for acts carried out on my orders. These acts were exclusively carried out for the welfare of the German people and because of my oath to the Führer. Although I am responsible for these acts only to the German people and can be tried only before a German court, I am at the same time prepared to give all the necessary information demanded of me by this court and to tell the whole truth without recognizing the jurisdiction of this court. I must, however, most strongly reject the acceptance by me of responsibility for acts of other persons which were not known to me; of which, had I known them, I would have disapproved and which could not have been prevented by me anyway.'

The rest pleaded not guilty, except for Hess who said simply: *'Nein.'*

Lawrence said that he interpreted this as 'not guilty', which brought a rare moment of laughter to the court.

# CHAPTER FOUR

## *Justice Jackson*

Lead American prosecutor Jackson then spelt out the justification for bringing the trial. This was not a case of victor's justice.

'If these men are the first war leaders of a defeated nation to be prosecuted in the name of the law,' he said, 'they are also the first to be given a chance to plead for their lives in the name of the law.'

Hundreds of tons of German documents had been examined. These had been found in German Army headquarters and government buildings, and also in salt mines, buried in the ground, concealed behind false walls and hidden in other places thought to be secure from discovery. They included articles, letters, diaries and memorandums written by the accused, along with orders issued by them. The defendants were to be condemned out of their own mouths.

Jackson quoted from Streicher, saying in *Der Stürmer* in 1942: 'Not only is Germany not safe in the face of the Jews as long as one Jew lives in Europe, but also the Jewish question is hardly solved in Europe so long as Jews live in the rest of the world.'

'Of the 9,600,000 Jews who lived in Nazi-dominated Europe, 60 per cent are authoritatively estimated to have perished,' Jackson pointed out. 'Five million seven hundred thousand Jews are missing from the countries in which they formerly lived, and over 4,500,000 cannot be accounted for by the normal death rate nor by immigration; nor are they included among displaced persons. History does not record a crime ever perpetrated against so many victims or one ever carried out with such calculated cruelty.'

Then he read from Frank's diary: 'The Jews are a race which has to be eliminated; whenever we catch one, it is his end.'

Not only were these men out to kill all Jews worldwide,

## Opening the Prosecution

they were also in a criminal conspiracy to wage war. Reading from the minutes of a meeting in 1938 attended by Göring, Raeder, Neurath and others, Jackson showed that Hitler had announced that he had decided to make a lightning attack on Czechoslovakia and Austria; and in May 1939 Hitler had advised his staff 'to attack Poland at the first suitable opportunity. We cannot expect a repetition of the Czech affair. [Where Britain and France had backed down.] There will be war.'

It was clear that Hitler did not care about the legality of these actions. In the files of the German Navy staff was the 'Memorandum on Intensified Naval War', dated 15 October 1939, which said: 'If decisive successes are expected from any measure considered as a war necessity, it must be carried through even if it is not in agreement with international law.'

A directive written by Keitel showed German collusion with Japan before the attack on Pearl Harbor to 'establish and maintain a new order of things'. Ribbentrop's reports showed him urging Japan to join the war to 'hasten the victory'. And a captured memorandum from Hitler's headquarters, dated 29 October 1940, stated that: 'The Führer is at present occupied with the question of the occupation of the Atlantic islands with a view to the prosecution of war against America at a later date.'

In the Commando Order of 18 October 1942 Hitler had ordered that British commandos were 'to be slaughtered to the last man' after capture. Orders signed by Hess commanded the arrest or liquidation of enemy airmen and parachutists. Jackson also quoted from a letter about the fate of Soviet prisoners of war from Rosenberg to Keitel in February 1942: 'Of 3,600,000 prisoners of war, only several hundred thousand are still able to work fully ... The camp commanders have forbidden the civilian population to put food at the disposal of the prisoners, and they have rather let them starve to death ... when prisoners of war could no longer keep up on the march because of hunger and exhaustion, they were shot before the eyes of the horrified population, and the corpses were left. In numerous camps, no shelter for the prisoners of war was provided at all. They lay under the open sky during rain or snow. Even tools were not made available to dig holes or caves ... in various camps, all the "Asiatics" were shot.'

A secret report from Rosenberg's Reich Ministry of Eastern Territory revealed that: 'Sauckel's action has caused unrest among the civilians ... Russian girls were deloused by men, nude photos in forced positions were taken, women doctors were locked into freight cars for the pleasure of the transport commanders .... '

In a speech made on 25 January 1944, Frank, then governor-general of Poland, boasted: 'I have sent 1,300,000 Polish workers into the Reich.' Sauckel reported that 'out of the five million foreign workers who arrived in Germany not even 200,000 came voluntarily.' This fact was reported to Hitler, Speer, Goring and Keitel. Rosenberg's ministry ordered the enslavement of children aged ten to 14.

From a report of SS General Jürgen Stoop on the destruction of the Warsaw Ghetto, Jackson read: 'Jews usually left their hideouts, but frequently remained in the burning buildings and jumped out of the windows only when the heat became unbearable. They then tried to crawl with broken bones across the street .... '

He also referred to the inventories kept by Göring and Keitel of the artworks and other valuables they had looted. When justifying the legality of prosecuting the defendants, Jackson even quoted the German Military Code, which said: 'If the execution of a military order in the course of duty violates the criminal law, then the superior officer giving

*The clearing and destruction of the Warsaw Ghetto in 1943 was clearly a war crime – survivors faced the perpetrators at Nuremberg.*

the order will bear the sole responsibility therefor. However, the obeying subordinate will share the punishment of the participant: (1) if he has exceeded the order given to him, or (2) if it was within his knowledge that the order of his superior officer concerned an act by which it was intended to commit a civil or military crime or transgression.'

This litany of iniquity continued all day. This time, Göring made no pretence of indifference. Even Hess gave up reading and listened to the speech. When the tribunal adjourned at 5.15 pm, colleagues clustered around Jackson to congratulate him on his exposition, which the press called 'magnificent'.

### *Documentary evidence*
Colonel Robert Storey, executive trial counsel for the United States, then explained how the evidence had been gathered and collated. Assistant US prosecutor Ralph

## CHAPTER FOUR

Albrecht explained the complex structure of the Nazi Party and its integration with the apparatus of the state, while Major Frank Wallis presented evidence of the defendants' involvement.

Lawrence stepped in to ask whether copies of the briefs he had prepared had been given to the defence counsels. Wallis said that, in agreement with the established procedure, six copies had been placed in the defendants' document room. Lawrence said that, as the crime was conspiracy, each defendant must have a copy. Storey complained that producing so many copies would put an intolerable strain on his department, though in one case 250 copies of a document had been handed out to the press.

Lawrence made a ruling that, henceforth, instead of just quoting the reference numbers of documents they handed over, each would have to be read aloud so they would appear in the record. This slowed the presentation of the prosecution case to a crawl.

On the fifth day of the trial, another US assistant prosecutor, Sidney Alderman, began presenting evidence on the planning and waging of aggressive war. He displayed charts showing the Nazi invasion of Czechoslovakia, then read a paper written by General Jodl entitled 'Strategic Position in the Beginning of the Fifth Year of the War' and delivered to Nazi gauleiters – district governors – in Munich on 7 November 1943, which detailed Germany's attacks on the countries that surrounded it.

When Alderman tried to introduce a transcript of the interrogation of Raeder, Raeder's counsel, Dr Walter Siemers, objected to the use of transcripts of interrogations of witnesses or defendants where the defence counsel had not been present. Lawrence conceded that copies should be given to the defence counsels and that, if the defence wanted to challenge evidence gained from the interrogation of the

## Opening the Prosecution

defendants, they would have an opportunity to do so if the defendant chose to take the witness stand.

### The film

It seemed that the court case was going to get bogged down with procedural considerations until, on the afternoon of the eighth day, the lights were lowered except for a single spotlight picking out the defendants and a film was shown of the liberation of the concentration camps. These images of men and women reduced to walking skeletons, the disfigured bodies of women who had survived medical experiments, the piles of bodies and the gas chambers and crematoria are still profoundly shocking more than 70 years after the event. Even counsel who had read detailed accounts of the atrocities were horrified.

Many preferred to watch the reaction of the defendants rather than the film. Ribbentrop, von Papen and Schacht turned away. Dönitz covered his eyes. Hess seemed to be mesmerized, while the virulent anti-Semite Streicher watched avidly, nodding his head. Göring remained calm, but by the end he was seen repeatedly wiping his sweaty palms.

When the film was over, Lawrence rushed from the room without adjourning the session. The room remained in a stunned silence until one journalist murmured: 'Why can't we shoot the swine now?' Then a soldier said: 'God, this makes me feel like killing the first German I meet.'

Hess was the first of the defendants to speak.

'I don't believe it,' he said. Göring silenced him.

Frank sat in silence for ten minutes until the guard came to take him back to his cell.

### Prison psychiatrist

Dr Gustav Gilbert, the prison psychiatrist, visited the defendants in their cells to judge their reaction. Göring, who had previously told Gilbert that all the atrocities had been carried out by Himmler and 'his chosen psychopaths', was trying to pull himself together. That morning, he had revelled in the limelight when the transcript of his telephone call directing the march into Austria had been read out.

'Everyone was laughing with me,' he said, 'and then they showed that awful film and it just spoiled everything.'

'It was those dirty SS swine,' said Keitel, saying he would never have let his son join the SS if he had known. Nevertheless, he managed to eat a hearty supper that night.

Through his tears, Fritzsche said: 'No power in heaven or earth will erase this shame from my country.'

Sauckel said: 'I'd choke myself with these hands if I thought I had the slightest thing to do with these murders.'

Jodl, Dönitz and Neurath also denied that they knew anything about it. But Frank was unapologetic.

'Don't let anyone tell you that they had no idea,' he said. 'Everybody sensed that there was something horribly wrong ... even if we didn't know all the details. They didn't want to know. It was too comfortable to live on the system, to support our families in royal style, and to believe that it was all right.'

### *First witness*

Jackson capitalized on the impact of the film with his first witness – Major General Erwin Lahousen. Originally with Austrian intelligence, Lahousen had been transferred after the Anschluss to the Abwehr (German military intelligence), where he had been assistant to its chief, Admiral Canaris. Not only could he talk in detail about the murder of civilians, the maltreatment of prisoners of war and the trick Keitel had ordered to provoke war – attacking the German radio station at Gleiwitz in 1939, leaving behind the corpses of concentration camp inmates in Polish uniforms – he could tie other defendants to these crimes.

He directly implicated Keitel, Ribbentrop and various officers in the High Command in drawing up the orders to kill all commandos, the instructions to the Einsatzkommando and the maltreatment of captured Soviet soldiers.

Before he took the stand, Gilbert had already asked Lahousen about his motives for testifying. Lahousen pointed out that Canaris and his immediate circle had been summarily executed after the failed Valkyrie plot to kill Hitler on 20 July 1944.

'I have to speak for those they murdered,' he said. 'I am the only one left.'

Keitel and Jodl were furious that such 'treacherous statements' should come from a serving officer. Göring said: 'That traitor – that's one we forgot on 20 July.'

Concerned only for his own skin, Ribbentrop trembled as he said: 'What shall I do?'

Keitel's attorney Otto Nelte protested that they had not been warned that Lahousen would be called, even though the press had been informed. Jackson argued that the tactic of pulling a rabbit from a hat was common in American courts. Besides, they were trying the case in a hotbed of Nazism and prosecution witnesses were in danger of their lives.

The best the defence could come up with was to ask Lahousen why, if he thought the orders Keitel was issuing were 'murderous' and thus criminal, he did not go to the police. Göring was exasperated by this inept line of questioning. His attorney Dr Stahmer asked whether the defendants could question the witness. The request was denied.

## *Legally sane*
After Lahousen's testimony, there was a private session to determine whether Hess was legally sane. He had been

## CHAPTER FOUR

found goose-stepping around the courtyard and appeared not to recognize his old friend Göring. While his attorney argued that he was unfit to stand trial, Lawrence asked Hess to speak.

He admitted to 'simulating loss of memory for tactical reasons ... in consultations with my officially appointed defence counsel, who has, therefore, represented me in good faith'. The tribunal then judged him to be sane.

But Dr Gilbert was unconvinced. He believed that Hess had only said this because he was afraid that, if found insane, he would be taken away from the other defendants. He had been alone in a British prison for much of the war. Now he was back among old colleagues, he was enjoying speaking his native German again.

Gilbert shared this with the press, allowing the American military newspaper *Stars and Stripes* to run the headline: 'Hess Nuts. Fake Story Fake, says Nuremberg Psychologist.'

## Chapter Five
# 'No Mere Willing Tools'

Sir Hartley Shawcross's opening statement for the British dealt with the charges of waging aggressive war. He directly addressed the argument that this had not been a crime under international law prior to the trial. He cited the Covenant of the League of Nations, which spoke of 'the acceptance of obligations not to resort to war', the Geneva Protocol of 1924 and the Kellogg-Briand Pact of 1928, which sought to outlaw war, along with numerous agreements between individual nations, many of which Germany had signed.

The Nazis had also signed the German-Soviet Non-Aggression Pact, which they had then cynically broken. But no mention of this could be made. Rudenko insisted that Stalin had seen through Hitler's double-dealing all along. Jackson remarked that the Russians 'didn't mind being called knaves as long as they weren't called fools'.

Nevertheless, Shawcross maintained that clearly the crime of aggressive war mentioned in the London Charter was not retroactive, but merely filled 'a gap in criminal procedure'. He went on to argue that the responsibility of waging an aggressive war lay not just with Hitler. The defendants were 'no mere willing tools'.

'They were the men whose support built Hitler up into the position of power he occupied,' Shawcross said. 'These are the men whose initiative and planning often conceived and certainly made possible the acts of aggression done in

Hitler's name; and these are the men who enabled Hitler to build up the army, the navy, the air force, the war economy, the political philosophy, by which these treacherous acts were carried out.'

After this opening speech, Shawcross had to go back to London. Maxwell Fyfe took over, introducing the various treaties in just four hours. US prosecutor Sidney Alderman then outlined the case that, in collaboration with Italy and Japan, the Germans had waged aggressive war against the United States.

### The Nazi plan

To reinforce the points made by Shawcross and Alderman, day 17 of the trial was given over almost entirely to viewing captured German films showing the Nazi Plan. The screening was divided into four parts – The Rise of the NSDAP, 1921–33; Acquiring Control of Germany, 1933–5; Preparation for Wars of Aggression, 1935–9; and Wars of Aggression, 1939–44.

These films implicated the defendants individually. Hess was shown making a speech, crying: 'The Party is the Führer and the Führer is Germany.'

Göring relished seeing himself on screen and shouted out the names of pilots and aircraft he recognized. Dönitz joined in with the names of seamen.

In a sequence showing the German economic recovery, Schacht beamed and said: 'Can you see anything wrong with that?' Schirach became excited when he saw his Hitler Youth marching past a parade stand. And when Hitler was shown in a full frenzy of oration, Göring dug Hess in the ribs and said: 'Justice Jackson will want to join the Party now.'

However, they fell silent during a sequence showing the suspects in the 20 July plot being physically dragged before a people's court with army officers struggling to hold up their beltless trousers. When one tries to describe murders he has seen in Poland, Judge Roland Freisler screams: 'Are you collapsing under the stress of your own vulgarity, you filthy rogue?'

Some were tried in the very room where the defendants were now sitting, before being hustled out to be shot, beheaded or hanged, often slowly, using piano wire. The contrast between Nazi justice and that being exercised by the tribunal could not have been more vividly portrayed.

*Film of Nazi judge Roland Freisler administering summary justice to the 20 July plotters contrasted with the meticulous protocols of the Nuremberg Trials.*

### *Forced labour*
The US prosecutors then turned to the conspiracy charges

## CHAPTER FIVE

concerning crimes against humanity and federal prosecutor Thomas Dodd made a two-day presentation on the use of forced labour. He quoted a letter from Sauckel to Rosenberg, dated 20 April 1942, saying: 'The aim of this new gigantic labour mobilization is to use all the rich and tremendous sources conquered and secured for us ... for the armament of the Armed Forces and also for the nutrition of the homeland. The raw materials as well as the fertility of the conquered territories and their human labour power are to be used completely and conscientiously to the profit of Germany and her allies.'

Dodd presented evidence that some 4,795,000 people were enslaved in the most brutal fashion. He read the speech of Erich Koch, Reichskommissar of the Ukraine, to a party meeting in 1943, in which he said: 'I will draw the very last out of this country. I did not come to spread bliss. I have come to help the Führer. The population must work, work and work again ... We are the master race, which must remember that the lowest German worker is racially and biologically a thousand times more valuable than the population here.'

In March 1944 Sauckel had told the Central Planning Board that he had trained French men and women to hunt for workers. They were then paid to ply candidates with liquor and dupe them, 'just as it was done in olden times for shanghaiing'. And in his diary, Frank, governor-general of Poland, wrote that he had 'no objections to all the rubbish, capable of work yet often loitering about, being snatched from the streets'. People were simply seized and taken to camps. Their families and friends rarely knew what had happened to them.

Dodd showed that the daily rations in a typical arms factory were a cup of tea at 4 am, with a bowl of soup and two slices of bread at the end of a 14-hour shift. An affidavit

## 'No Mere Willing Tools'

signed by a doctor at one of Krupp's labour camps, in Essen, said workers were fed 1,000 calories a day – less than the minimum prescribed for a German. They were fed condemned meat infected with tuberculosis and were riddled with fleas and lice. If they fell ill, there were few medical supplies. Even so, the conditions there were better than in SS labour camps where Himmler had decreed that Jews, gypsies, Poles, Russians and Ukrainians must suffer 'extermination through work'.

Dodd also presented evidence of mass executions and the use of gas vans and gas chambers. He presented Eichmann's reporting of the death of 4 million Jews in concentration camps, plus another 2 million at the hands of the police in the East. The death books from Mauthausen concentration camp were presented. They showed that, on one day in March 1945, 203 people had died at regular intervals from 'heart attacks' in alphabetical order. The documents Dodd produced overwhelmed the tribunal and Lawrence begged him to stop.

### *Concentration camps*

Dodd changed tack and held up the shrunken head of a Polish officer, which camp commandant Karl Koch had used as a paperweight. The victim had apparently been hanged for a sexual encounter with a German woman. Dodd also showed the skin of prisoners that had been tattooed, then flayed from them and handed over to Koch's wife, Ilse, to make lampshades. This was supported by an affidavit from Koch.

Kaltenbrunner had now joined the others in the dock and, Kaufmann, his counsel, objected. The prosecution had failed to mention that Koch had already been executed by firing squad. It transpired that Koch had been shot for embezzlement and the murder of a camp doctor and medical orderly who had treated him for syphilis. Ilse Koch – The Beast of Buchenwald – had been captured by the Americans in 1945. Sentenced to life in 1947, she was released, but re-arrested and sentenced to life again by a German court. She hanged herself in prison in 1967.

More German footage was shown. This time it was the amateur film of an SS guard showing naked girls running, and naked men and women being kicked and beaten by German soldiers while the SS looked on.

### Persecution and Germanization
The following day, the US delegation continued its presentation, focusing on the persecution and murder of Jews, particularly in the occupied parts of the Soviet Union. That Friday, when the defendants returned to their cells, all except for Schacht were said to be resigned to death, though they continued to blame others for the atrocities they had now witnessed.

The youthful Captain Sam Harris was brought in to present the case on the forcible Germanization of the occupied territories. He began his speech with the words: 'My knees haven't knocked so much since I asked my wonderful little wife to marry me.'

Birkett was aghast, saying: 'The shocking bad taste is really unbelievable.' Biddle just said, 'Jesus,' then gave the young attorney a dressing-down in private.

### Colonel Storey
In the week before Christmas, Colonel Robert Storey took over again. He introduced the 39 volumes of photographs of the works of art seized by Rosenberg's 'special task force'.

It then fell to Storey to present evidence against the Leadership Corps of the Nazi Party. He did this with a blizzard of documents. Lawrence and Biddle could not see the relevance of many of them. When Storey conceded that one 'might be considered strictly cumulative,' he was told: 'Well, if it's cumulative, we don't really want to hear it.'

Dönitz went to sleep, while the others nudged each other and laughed each time Storey was reprimanded. He handled the case so badly that some colleagues unkindly dubbed him the 'Butcher of Nuremberg'.

Storey's case against the Reich cabinet should have proved more promising as all the defendants – apart from Fritzsche, Sauckel, Schirach and Streicher – had been members. However, it had not met after 1937 and was not relevant to the crimes they had been charged with.

Next Storey also presented the case against the SA. However, after the 'Night of the Long Knives' in June 1934, when Hitler had used the SS to murder Ernst Röhm and other potential rivals among the Brownshirts, the SA had ceased to play any major political role in Nazi affairs.

Major Warren Farr was no more effective in beginning the case against the SS as, once again, the groundwork had to be laid with a plethora of documentation. Storey returned to lay the basis of the case against the Gestapo and the SD.

### *Hermann Gräbe*

On 2 January, Storey resumed after the Christmas recess with an affidavit given by Hermann Gräbe, a German engineer with the firm Jung A.G. who had witnessed a massacre in Dubno in the Ukraine on 2 October 1942. Part of it read:

> *I drove to the site ... and saw near it great mounds of earth, about 30 metres long and 2 metres high. Several trucks stood in front of the mounds. Armed Ukrainian militia drove the people off the trucks under the supervision of an SS man. The militia men acted as guards*

## CHAPTER FIVE

*on the trucks and drove them to and from the pit. All these people had the regulation yellow patches on the front and back of their clothes, and thus could be recognized as Jews .... My foreman and I went directly to the pits. Nobody bothered us. Now I heard rifle shots in quick succession from behind one of the earth mounds. The people who had got off the trucks – men, women and children of all ages – had to undress upon the order of an SS man who carried a riding or dog whip. They had to put down their clothes in fixed places, sorted according to shoes, top clothing and undergarments. I saw heaps of shoes of about 800 to 1000 pairs, great piles of under-linen and clothing. Without screaming or weeping these people undressed, stood around in family groups, kissed each other, said farewells, and waited for a sign from another SS man, who stood near the pit, also with a whip in his hand. During the fifteen minutes I stood near, I heard no complaint or plea for mercy. I watched a family of about eight persons, a man and a woman both of about fifty, with their children of about twenty to twenty-four, and two grown-up daughters about twenty-eight or twenty-nine. An old woman with snow-white hair was holding a one-year-old child in her arms and singing to it and tickling it. The child was cooing with delight. The parents were looking on with tears in their eyes. The father was holding the hand of a boy about ten years old and speaking to him softly; the boy was fighting his tears. The father pointed to the sky, stroked his head and seemed to explain something to him. At that moment the SS man at the pit started shouting something to his comrade. The latter counted off about twenty persons and instructed them to go behind the earth mound. Among them was the family I have just*

## 'No Mere Willing Tools'

*mentioned. I well remember a girl, slim with black hair, who, as she passed me, pointed to herself and said, 'Twenty-three years old.' I walked around the mound and found myself confronted by a tremendous grave. People were closely wedged together and lying on top of each other so that only their heads were visible. Nearly all had blood running over their shoulders from their heads. Some of the people shot were still moving. Some were lifting their arms and turning their heads to show that they were still alive. The pit was nearly two-thirds full. I estimated that it already contained about a thousand people. I looked for the man who did the shooting. He was an SS man, who sat at the edge of the narrow end of the pit, his feet dangling into the pit. He had a tommy-gun on his knees and was smoking a cigarette. The people, completely naked, went down some steps, which were cut in the clay wall of the pit, and clambered over the heads of the people lying there to the place to which the SS man directed them. They lay down in front of the dead or wounded people; some caressed those who were still alive and spoke to them in a low voice. Then I heard a series of shots. I looked into the pit and saw that the bodies were twitching or the heads lying already motionless on top of the bodies that lay beneath them. Blood was running from their necks. The next batch was approaching already. They went down into the pit, lined themselves up against the previous victims and were shot.*

This testimony was used again in the Einsatzgruppen trial that followed. There again, it proved crucial.

### Otto Ohlendorf

SS Lieutenant General Otto Ohlendorf was brought in to

## CHAPTER FIVE

give testimony against Kaltenbrunner, having served under him in the Reich Main Security Office (RSHA), the principal body of Himmler's state security apparatus. During Operation Barbarossa, the invasion of the Soviet Union, Ohlendorf had been in command of Einsatzgruppe D. Asked how many his death squad had killed, he replied: 'In the year between June 1941 to June 1942 the Einsatzkommandos reported ninety thousand people liquidated.'

The counsel for the SS, Ludwig Babel, asked: 'Was the legality of the orders explained to those people under false pretences?'

Ohlendorf was puzzled.

'I do not understand your question,' he said, 'since the order was issued by the superior authorities, the question

*Witness Otto Ohlendorf takes the stand, while Heinz Jost listens via headphones. Both men were later defendants in the Einsatzgruppen Trial. Ohlendorf was hanged. Jost was later pardoned and released.*

## 'No Mere Willing Tools'

of legality could not arise in the minds of these individuals, for they had sworn obedience to the people who had issued the orders.'

He had no scruples about carrying out these orders, 'because to me it is inconceivable that a subordinate leader should not carry out orders given by the leaders of the state,' he said. He sent some men home because he did not consider them 'emotionally suitable' to execute these tasks. No one could disobey – 'the result would have been a court martial with a corresponding sentence'.

Ohlendorf was tried and convicted in the Einsatzgruppen trial in 1948 and hanged in 1951.

### Dieter Wisliceny

SS Captain Dieter Wisliceny had been Eichmann's deputy. Given the task of transporting Slovakian Jews to Auschwitz, he requested verification of the order. Eichmann took a letter from his safe, written by Himmler. It said: 'The Führer has ordered the final solution of the Jewish question.' Wisliceny was then asked what 'final solution' meant.

'Eichmann told me that the words "final solution" meant the biological extermination of the Jewish race,' Wisliceny said. 'I was so much impressed with this document which gave Eichmann authority to kill millions of people that I said at the time: "May God forbid that our enemies should ever do anything similar to the German people." He replied: "Don't be sentimental – this is a Führer order." ... The programme of extermination was already under way and continued until late 1944. There was no change in the programme during Kaltenbrunner's administration.'

Eichmann had been cold-blooded about the outcome. According to Wisliceny: 'He said to me on the occasion of our last meeting in February 1945, at which time we were discussing our fates upon losing the war: "I laugh when I jump into the grave because of the feeling that I have killed five million Jews. That gives me great satisfaction and gratification.'"

Wisliceny was so frank in the testimony that he had given in his affidavit that neither the prosecutors nor defence counsels could find any questions to ask him. He was tried in Czechoslovakia and hanged in February 1948.

### Bach-Zelewski

Colonel Telford Taylor presented the case against the German general staff and high command. He concentrated on the Barbarossa Order issued by Keitel to German forces shortly before the invasion of the Soviet Union. One of its directives was: 'Guerrillas should be disposed of ruthlessly by the military.'

Taylor called to the stand SS Obergruppenführer Erich von dem Bach-Zelewski, whose ruthlessness Hitler had praised. Biddle said he looked like 'a mild and rather serious accountant'.

'My principal task was fighting partisans,' he said.

At the end of 1942, he became the Chief of Anti-Partisan Combat Units for the entire Eastern Front. Most of the anti-partisan operations were not undertaken by SS fanatics, but by ordinary army units, and he confirmed that orders were issued by the highest authorities that German soldiers committing excesses were not to be punished in the military courts.

This caused consternation among the defendants. Göring called Bach-Zelewski 'the bloodiest murderer of the whole damn set-up'. Asked for an explanation of this widespread barbarity by Rosenberg's counsel, Bach-Zelewski replied: 'If for years, for decades, a doctrine is preached to the effect that the Slav race is an inferior race, and that Jews are not even human beings, then an explosion of this sort is inevitable.'

The responsibility was not his alone, but was spread throughout the Wehrmacht. Everyone had taken part.

Taylor hammered home the point: 'The general staff and high command group planned and carried through manifold acts of aggression which turned Europe into a charnel house and caused the armed forces to be used for foul practices, foully executed, of terror, pillage, and wholesale slaughter.'

Bach-Zelewski said he disapproved of Himmler's plan to exterminate 30 million Slavs. He said he tried to temper policies where he could and could not resign as 'if someone else had been in my position the disaster would have been greater'.

He was never prosecuted for war crimes and did not serve time in prison until 1958, when he was given four-and-a-half years for murdering an SA officer on the 'Night of the Long Knives' in 1934. He was later given an additional ten years for murdering ten German communists in the 1930s and died in prison in 1972.

# Chapter Six
# Presenting the Evidence

When the prosecution began making the case against individual defendants, they excluded Kaltenbrunner, Sauckel and Speer, feeling that their guilt had already been sufficiently established by the evidence given in the general charges.

The American delegation then began with Göring, presenting documents on his participation in the Munich Putsch in 1923 and the use of concentration amp inmates in his aircraft factories.

### Rosenberg

Next came Rosenberg. The son of a Lithuanian father and Estonian mother, he had spelt out his racial theories in a book of Nordic ramblings called *The Myth of the Twentieth Century*. Second to *Mein Kampf* as a bible of Nazism, it sold over a million copies, though Schirach said Rosenberg had 'sold more copies of a book that no one ever read than any other author'. Goebbels dismissed the book as an 'ideological belch'.

Although Rosenberg had already been implicated in the wholesale looting of artworks, the main emphasis of the submission made by US assistant prosecutor Walter W. Brudno, who had been a private, first class in the US Army until two weeks before the presentation, had to do with Rosenberg's establishment of the Institute for the Exploration of the Jewish Question. Brudno read the statement Rosenberg made at its opening: 'For Germany the Jewish question is

## Presenting the Evidence

*During breaks, defendants were allowed to talk.
Left to right: Rudolf Hess, Alfred Rosenberg, Hans Frank,
Franz von Pappen, Wilhelm Frick and Albert Speer.*

only then solved when the last Jew has left the Greater German space. Since Germany with its blood and its folkdom has now broken for always this Jewish dictatorship for all Europe and has seen to it that Europe as a whole will become free from the Jewish parasitism once more, we may, I believe, also say for all Europeans: For Europe the Jewish question is only then solved when the last Jew has left the European continent.'

Brudno went on to show that during his time as Reichminister for the Occupied Eastern Territories Rosenberg had put these policies into action.

### *Frank and Streicher*
Hitler's personal lawyer, Frank had handed over to his American captors 42 leather-bound volumes of his personal

diaries, thinking his criticism of Hitler in them would exonerate him. Instead they were offered as evidence for the prosecution. One extract read: 'Before the German people suffer starvation, the occupied territories and their people shall be exposed to starvation. This means a six-fold increase over that of last year's contribution .... It must be done cold-bloodedly and without pity.' Evidence about the ill-treatment and murder of Jews during the time he was governor-general of Poland was also entered.

The British delegation outlined the case against Streicher. Again he had condemned himself with his own pen – through his writings in propaganda newspaper *Der Stürmer*. In January 1937, Himmler wrote that future history would state 'that Julius Streicher and his weekly *Der Stürmer* would have contributed a great deal towards the enlightenment regarding the enemy of humanity (the Jews).' But he had no public post after 1940.

## *Schacht and Funk*

As president of the Reichsbank and minister of economics, Schacht had put an end to runaway inflation. The case against him was that he had helped Hitler to power, knew of his aggressive aims and organized the foreign loans that had financed rearmament. But the prosecution case was thin: Schacht had distanced himself from the Nazi regime after 1937 and, following the 20 July plot in 1944, he had been arrested and sent to Ravensbrück concentration camp.

His successor, Funk, had organized the funding of the Nazi Party and, as president of the Reichsbank, he had arranged for the gold teeth of murdered Jews and money raised from other stolen valuables to be paid into false accounts. Nevertheless Colonel Andrus said he was 'incapable of running a gas station'.

### Presenting the Evidence

## *Dr Franz Blaha*

At this point, the first inmate of a concentration camp was called. Dr Franz Blaha, a Czech, had been interned in Dachau from April 1941 until the camp was liberated in April 1945. When he refused to perform operations on 20 healthy patients, he was sent to the autopsy room where he performed 12,000 post-mortems. He was examined on his affidavit, which said:

*From the middle of 1941 to the end of 1942 some 500 operations on healthy prisoners were performed. These were for the instructions of the SS medical students and doctors and included operations on the stomach, gall bladder and throat. These were performed by students and doctors of only two years' training, although they were very dangerous and difficult. Ordinarily they would not have been done except by surgeons with at least four years' surgical practice. Many prisoners died on the operating table and many others from later complications. I performed autopsies on all of these bodies ....*

*During my time at Dachau I was familiar with many kinds of medical experiments carried on there on human victims. These persons were never volunteers but were forced to submit to such acts. Malaria experiments on about 1,200 people were conducted by Dr Klaus Schilling between 1941 and 1945. Schilling was personally ordered by Himmler to conduct these experiments. The victims were either bitten by mosquitoes or given injections of malaria sporozoites taken from mosquitoes .... Thirty to forty died from the malaria itself. Three hundred to four hundred died later from diseases which were fatal because of the physical condition resulting from the malaria attacks. In addition*

# CHAPTER SIX

*there were deaths resulting from poisoning due to overdoses of neosalvarsan and pyramidon ....*

*In 1942 and 1943 experiments on human beings were conducted by Dr Sigmund Rascher to determine the effects of changing air pressure. As many as 25 persons were put at one time into a specially constructed van in which pressure could be increased or decreased as required .... Most of the prisoners used died from these experiments, from internal haemorrhage of the lungs or brain. The survivors coughed blood when taken out. It was my job to take the bodies out and as soon as they were found to be dead to send the internal organs to Munich for study. About 400 to 500 prisoners were experimented on. The survivors were sent to invalid blocks and liquidated shortly afterwards.*

*Rascher also conducted experiments on the effect of cold water on human beings. This was done to find a way for reviving airmen who had fallen into the ocean. The subject was placed in ice cold water and kept there until he was unconscious .... Some men stood it as long as 24 to 36 hours. The lowest body temperature reached was 19 degrees centigrade, but most men died at 25 or 26 degrees. When the men were removed from the ice water attempts were made to revive them by artificial sunshine, with hot water, by electro-therapy, or by animal warmth. For this last experiment prostitutes were used and the body of the unconscious man was placed between the bodies of two women. Himmler was present at one such experiment .... About 300 persons were used in these experiments. The majority died. Of those who survived, many became mentally deranged. Those who did not die were sent to invalid blocks and were killed just as were the victims of the air pressure experiments ....*

> *Liver puncture experiments were performed by Dr Brachtl on healthy people and on people who had diseases of the stomach and gall bladder. For this purpose a needle was jabbed into the liver of a person and a small piece of the liver was extracted. No anaesthetic was used ....*

The catalogue of barbarity continued throughout his testimony. Healthy men – usually Polish, Czech or Dutch priests – were injected with pus from diseased people. Half were treated, some having limbs amputated, though Blaha's autopsies revealed that chemical treatments were also harmful. Between 600 and 800 people died. Others became permanent invalids and were later killed.

'It was common practice to remove the skin from dead prisoners,' said Dr Blaha. 'Human skin from human backs and chests ... was chemically treated and placed in the sun to dry. After that it was cut into various sizes for use as saddles, riding breeches, gloves, house slippers, and ladies' handbags. Tattooed skin was especially valued by SS men. Russians, Poles, and other inmates were used in this way, but it was forbidden to cut out the skin of a German. This skin had to be from healthy prisoners and free from defects. Sometimes we did not have enough bodies with good skin and Rascher would say, "All right, you will get the bodies." The next day we would receive 20 or 30 bodies of young people. They would have been shot in the neck or struck on the head so that the skin would be uninjured.'

Skeleton and skulls, particularly those with good teeth, were in demand by SS men. Blaha would have to boil off the flesh and bleach them. There was evidence of cannibalism in the transports that brought fresh inmates. Blaha's autopsies showed that the victims had died from suffocation or lack of water. Sometimes transports were left in a siding so everyone starved to death.

Blaha also performed autopsies on the victims of the gas chamber at Dachau. He also told of the appalling treatment of prisoners of war and their deliberate murder, the epidemics and the insanitary conditions. The sick were just shot in the neck, though after the camp was liberated he found plenty of medicine in the SS hospital.

## Consternation in the dock
This testimony caused consternation in the defendants' box, particularly when Blaha described visits to the camp by Bormann, Frick, Rosenberg, Funk, Sauckel and Kaltenbrunner. He picked out those he had seen personally from among the defendants in the dock.

The defence tried to trip Dr Blaha up over precise dates, but he had a remarkable memory and could not be faulted. What's more the guilt spread beyond those in the dock.

'In my opinion, the people who lived in the neighbourhood of Munich must have known of all these things, because the prisoners went every day to various factories in Munich and the neighbourhood; and at work they frequently came into contact with the civilian workers,' he said. 'Moreover, the various suppliers and consumers often entered the fields and the factories of the German armament works and they saw what was done to the prisoners and what they looked like.'

## Soldiers, sailors and diplomats
The British presented the cases against the soldiers, sailors and diplomats. The case against Dönitz focused on war crimes. The submission included calling two former German captains of U-boats who testified that an order from Dönitz had encouraged the killing of shipwrecked crew. It was also alleged that Dönitz 'was an extreme Nazi who did his utmost

to indoctrinate the Navy and the German people with the Nazi creed'.

As Grand Admiral and Commander-in-Chief of the German Navy until 1943, Raeder had overseen the rebuilding of the Kriegsmarine in the 1930s. Documentary evidence was presented that he had urged Hitler to invade and occupy Norway. He also passed on the Commando Order, which had led to the execution of British commandos by a German Navy firing squad.

Foreign minister von Neurath had been at the Hossbach Conference in 1937, where Hitler had outlined his expansionist plans. As Reichsprotektor of occupied Bohemia and Moravia, he had dissolved the Czech parliament, closed the universities, taken control of the press and instituted the Nuremberg race laws.

The case against Ribbentrop was largely a recapitulation of evidence that had already been heard. And little fresh could be said against von Papen apart from the fact that as ambassador to Vienna he had given assistance to Hitler over the annexation of Austria.

## Chapter Seven
# War Crimes

On 17 January 1946, six weeks after the beginning of the trial, François de Menthon rose to make his opening statement on behalf of the French delegation. He, too, cited the Kellogg-Briand Pact – initially signed by US Secretary of State Frank B. Kellogg and French foreign minister Aristide Briand – as a precedent. His case was heartfelt: three times in 50 years France had been invaded by Germany.

'The conscience of the peoples, who only yesterday were enslaved and tortured both in soul and body, calls upon you to judge and to condemn the most monstrous attempt at domination and barbarism of all times, both in the persons of some of those who bear the chief responsibility and in the collective groups and organizations which were the essential instruments of their crimes,' he told the tribunal. 'France, which was systematically plundered and ruined; France, so many of whose sons were tortured and murdered in the jails of the Gestapo or in concentration camps; France, which was subjected to the still more horrible grip of demoralization and return to barbarism diabolically imposed by Nazi Germany, asks you, above all in the name of the heroic martyrs of the Resistance, who are among the greatest heroes of our national legend, that justice be done.'

De Menthon concentrated on war crimes, which he categorized as economic looting, forced labour, crimes against persons and crimes against humankind. He concluded by expressing the hope that their judgment would be a decisive act in the history of international law and the foundation of a peaceful order. If that was the case, he said, 'the need for justice of the martyred peoples will be satisfied, and their sufferings will not have been useless to the progress of mankind'.

## Looting and forced labour

The French delegation then began presenting evidence of looting and forced labour, not just in France but also in Norway, Denmark, the Netherlands, Belgium and Luxembourg – countries whose cases had so far been under-represented.

The taking of forced labour was in violation of the Franco-German Armistice signed after the Nazi invasion in 1940 and the Hague Conventions, agreements on the conduct of war signed in 1899 and 1907. Documents from the Nazi archives showed that, by March 1943, some 250,000 civilians had been forced to build the Atlantic Wall in an attempt to prevent the anticipated Anglo-American invasion that occurred on D-Day the following year. More than 875,000 French labourers had been sent to work in Germany, along with 430,000 Dutch and 150,000 Belgians.

Assistant French prosecutor Jacques B. Herzog cited a report in which Sauckel admitted that there were 5 million foreign workers in Germany, of whom just 20,000 were volunteers. Production facilities in the occupied countries were also exploited. A report was read in which one German officer wrote: 'I attach the greatest importance to the proposition that the factories in the occupied territories, Holland, Belgium and France, be utilized as much as possible to ease the strain on the German armament production and to increase war potential.'

## CHAPTER SEVEN

### Illegal seizures

Article 52 of the Convention on Laws and Customs of War on Land signed in The Hague in 1899 said: 'Neither requisitions in kind nor services can be demanded from communes or inhabitants except for the necessities of the army of occupation.'

This plainly had not been the case in the Second World War. From France alone, the maximum the Germans could have legally demanded for the maintenance of their army of occupation was 74,000 million francs. They had taken more than ten times that amount. In Belgium, the illegal seizure had amounted to 130,000 Belgian francs; in Denmark, 8,000 million crowns and 70 million crowns' worth of agricultural production had been seized each month.

The Netherlands had lost 875,000 farm animals, 28,950 freight cars, 1 million bicycles and 600,000 radios, plus 1,100 million guilders' worth of machinery and oil. Norway was down 300,000 tons of hay and straw, 13,000 tons of soap, 30,000 tons of meat, 61,000 tons of dairy produce, 26,000 tons of fish, 112,000 of fats and 68,000 tons of fruit and vegetables.

The average daily consumption in France had fallen from 3,000 calories a day at the beginning of the war to 900 calories a day. In the Netherlands it had fallen to 400 calories a day. Also entered into evidence was a speech by Göring who had boasted: 'If famine is to reign, it will not reign in Germany.'

### Night and fog

French civilians disappeared without warning and with no indication of what had happened to them. Some 29,000 hostages had been shot. Thousands had been tortured in 'protective custody'. Mass fines and reprisals were imposed for sabotage. In Denmark, Hitler ordered that five Danes be killed for every German. Between the beginning of 1944 and the end of the war, 267 prominent Danes had been killed in their homes and offices or on the street. Where the police caught the perpetrator, the killer got a letter of congratulation from Himmler.

*Partisan suspects being arrested in Brittany. Under the 'Night and Fog' decree they would be despatched to concentration camps. Few would return.*

In 1941 Keitel had signed the *Nacht und Nebel* – 'Night and Fog' – decree. Under this, persons in occupied territories engaging in activities intended to undermine the security of German troops were to be brought to Germany 'by night and fog' for trial by special courts, thus circumventing military procedure and various conventions governing the treatment of prisoners. Keitel's counsel objected on the grounds that the decree was not the words of his client. Deputy French prosecutor Charles Dubost responded by saying: 'I knew that the accused Keitel had signed it, but that Hitler had conceived it. Therefore, I made allusion to the military honour of this general, who was not afraid to become the lackey of Hitler.'

It was estimated that 6,000 Luxembourgers, 5,200 Danes, 5,400 Norwegians, 12,000 Dutch and 37,000 Belgians had been sent to concentration camps. Of the 250,000 French deported, only 35,000 returned home. Up to 25 per cent died on the transports on the way to the camps.

### Maurice Lampe

The French called Maurice Lampe, an inmate at the Mauthausen concentration camp, to testify to the conditions at the camp. After two-and-a-half years' internment in France, he was transported with 104 others in an unventilated cattle truck. Although it was 12 degrees below zero, they travelled naked. The journey took three days.

When they arrived at Mauthausen, an SS officer told the convoy of some 1,200 Frenchmen: 'Germany needs your arms. You are, therefore, going to work; but I want to tell you that you will never see your families again. When one enters this camp, one leaves it by the chimney of the crematorium.'

Lampe detailed some scenes he found particularly horrible. Forty-seven British, American and Dutch airmen were made to undress. One American officer asked that he should be allowed to meet his death as a soldier. He was beaten with a whip. They were then marched to a quarry.

'At the bottom of the steps they loaded stone on the backs of these poor men and they had to carry them to the top,' said Lampe. 'The first journey was made with stones weighing 25 to 30 kilos and was accompanied by blows. Then they were made to run down. For the second journey the stones were still heavier; and whenever the poor wretches sank under their burden, they were kicked and hit with a bludgeon, even stones were hurled at them.

'This went on for several days. In the evening when I returned from the gang with which I was then working, the road which led to the camp was a bath of blood. I almost stepped on the lower jaw of a man. Twenty-one bodies were strewn along the road. Twenty-one had died on the first day. The twenty-six others died the following morning.'

Lampe testified that Himmler had visited Mauthausen to witness the shooting of 50 Soviet prisoners of war.

'I saw these Soviet officers lined up in rows of five in front of my block,' he said. 'They were called one by one, and there was a sort of human chain between the group which was awaiting its turn and that which was in the stairway listening to the shots which killed their predecessors. They were all killed by a shot in the neck.'

Another 400 prisoners had been killed because the camp was overcrowded. They had survived a convoy on which 800 had died, only to be stripped naked and left outside when the temperature was 18 degrees below zero. When they did not die fast enough, they were drenched with freezing water. The last of them were finished off with axes.

## *Madame Vaillant-Couturier*

Picked up by the Vichy French police, Marie-Claude Vaillant-Couturier had been sent to Auschwitz in 1942. She described a roll call on 5 February 1943:

> *In the morning at 3.30 the whole camp was awakened and sent out on the plain, whereas normally the roll call was at 3.30 but inside the camp. We remained out in front of the camp until five in the afternoon, in the snow, without any food. Then when the signal was given we had to go through the door one by one, and we were struck in the back with a cudgel, each one of us, in order to make us run. Those who could not run,*

## CHAPTER SEVEN

*either because they were too old or too ill, were caught by a hook and taken to Block 25, 'waiting block' for the gas chamber. On that day, ten of the French women of our convoy were thus caught and taken to Block 25.*

*When all the internees were back in the camp, a party to which I belonged was organized to go and pick up the bodies of the dead which were scattered over the plain as on a battlefield. We carried to the yard of Block 25 the dead and the dying without distinction, and they remained there stacked up in a pile ... from time to time a hand or a head would stir among the bodies, trying to free itself. It was a dying woman attempting to get free and live. The rate of mortality in that block was even more terrible than elsewhere because, having been condemned to death, they received food or drink only if there was something left in the cans in the kitchen; which means that very often they went for several days without a drop of water.*

*One of our companions, Annette Epaux, a fine young woman of 30, passing the block one day, was overcome with pity for those women who moaned from morning till night in all languages, 'Drink. Drink. Water!' She came back to our block to get a little herbal tea, but as she was passing it through the bars of the window she was seen by the Aufseherin [guard], who took her by the neck and threw her into Block 25. All my life I will remember Annette Epaux. Two days later I saw her on the truck which was taking the internees to the gas chamber. She had her arms around another French woman, old Line Porcher, and when the truck started moving she cried, 'Think of my little boy, if you ever get back to France.' Then they started singing 'The Marseillaise'.*

*In Block 25, in the courtyard, there were rats as big*

*as cats running about and gnawing the corpses and even attacking the dying who had not enough strength left to chase them away.*

She was cross-examined by the counsel for Streicher, who only succeeded in eliciting that just 50 of the 230 women sent to Auschwitz survived.

## Medical experiments

Dr Victor Dupont described the interrogations at Buchenwald. There was, he said, 'every imaginable kind of beating, immersion in bathtubs, squeezing of testicles, hanging, crushing of the head in iron bands, and the torturing of entire families in each others' sight. I have, in particular, seen a wife tortured before her husband; and children were tortured before their mothers.'

There were medical experiments and mass murders, particularly of Jews and gypsies. Their ashes were thrown in the excrement pit or used to fertilize the surrounding fields.

Towards the end of the war, as the Allies advanced, the camp commandant promised to hand over the keys of the camp.

'I do not want any atrocities,' he said.

When the Allied advance was held up, a delegation of prisoners went to see him to remind him that he had given 'his word of honour as a soldier'.

'He seemed acutely embarrassed,' said Dr Dupont, 'and explained that Sauckel, the governor of Thuringia, had given orders that no prisoner should remain in Buchenwald.'

Dr Alfred Balachowsky also testified about the medical experiments at Buchenwald.

'The human beings subjected to experiments were recruited, not only in the Buchenwald Camp, but also outside the camp. They were not volunteers; in most cases they did not know that they would be used for experiments until they entered Block 46,' he said. 'For the greater part they were of no service to science. Therefore, they can hardly be called experiments. The men were used for observing the effects of drugs, poisons, bacterial cultures, etc. .... They were literally murdered to keep typhus germs alive.'

## *Proved over and over again*

Norwegian Hans Cappelen testified about being tortured by the Gestapo in Oslo. He was beaten with rubber bludgeons and iron cable ends, until he fainted and was revived with ice-cold water.

'Then they started to beat me again, but it was useless to beat a man like me who was so swollen up and looking so bad. Then they started in another way, they started to screw and break my arms and legs. And my right arm was dislocated .... Then they placed a sort of home-made — it looked to me like a sort of home-made wooden thing, with a screw arrangement, on my left leg; and they started to screw so that all the flesh loosened from the bones. I felt an awful pain and fainted away again.'

The French continued presenting witnesses until *The Times* complained that the trial was 'being surfeited by the most murderous and revolting record of all time'. Birkett said that 'from the point of view of the trial it is a complete waste of time. The case has been proved over and over again. Neither does the world need it any more, for all over the world the evidence has been published ... but it seems impossible to stop it, or to check the volumes of it.'

## Chapter Eight
# Devastation in the East

On 8 February 1946, Rudenko began his opening speech on war crimes and crimes against humanity in the east. Göring and Hess took off their headphones as if to show that there was nothing worth listening to.

Rudenko, too, justified the establishment of the tribunal in international law and condemned the theory of racial superiority by which the defendants claimed the right to act as they did.

'For the first time in the history of mankind is justice confronted with crimes committed on so vast a scale, with crimes which have entailed such grave consequences,' he said. 'It is the first time that criminals who have seized an entire state and made this state an instrument of their monstrous crimes appear before a court of justice. It is also for the first time that, by judging these defendants, we sit in judgment not only of the defendants themselves, but also on the criminal institutions and organization which they created and on the inhuman theories and ideas which they promulgated ... '

Then he began to catalogue the damage the Nazis had wreaked in the east, which include the destruction of 1,670 Orthodox churches, 337 Catholic churches, 69 chapels, 532 synagogues. Some 1,710 cities and more than 70,000 villages had been almost completely razed, 6 million buildings ruined, including 51,850 industrial establishments, 40,000 hospitals, 84,000 schools and colleges, and 43,000 libraries.

## CHAPTER EIGHT

An estimated 25 million people were now homeless – and they had starved: the Nazis had removed or slaughtered 17 million head of cattle, 20 million pigs, 27 million sheep and goats, and 110 million poultry, along with 7 million horses.

Avoiding any mention of the Molotov-Ribbentrop Pact, the Soviet prosecutors also submitted statements from the governments of Poland, Czechoslovakia and Yugoslavia, although Maxwell Fyfe had already covered the invasios of these countries under crimes against peace.

*In Russia, German troops were encouraged to use particular brutality in their destruction of life and property. Villages were simply put to the torch.*

### Invasion of the Soviet Union
On the afternoon of 11 February, the Soviets caused a sensation by calling Field Marshal Friedrich Paulus, who had surrendered the German Sixth Army at Stalingrad, as a witness for the prosecution. When working for the chief of the army general staff earlier in his career, he had been ordered to draw up a full-scale plan for the invasion of the Soviet Union.

'The whole aim was conquest for the purpose of colonizing Russian territory; and by exploitation and looting them the war in the west was to be carried to an end, with the object of finally establishing supremacy over Europe,' he said.

The following day, he was subjected to a nine-hour cross-examination by the counsels for the defence. In it, he admitted that the plan to invade the Soviet Union was begun in the autumn of 1940.

'Already at that time you thought that that was Hitler's intention, didn't you?' asked Nelte.

'From the way in which this task was started one could see that, after the theoretical preparation, a practical application would follow,' Paulus replied.

He also admitted that the Abwehr had no indication that the Soviet Union was preparing to attack.

As the cross-examination went on, Paulus began to say he had forgotten certain details and Göring quipped contemptuously: 'Hess, do you know you've got a competitor.'

### *Treatment of prisoners of war*

The Soviet prosecutors read the order given by the German High Command to the army in January 1942: 'All clemency or humaneness towards prisoners of war is strictly condemned. A German soldier must always make his prisoners feel his superiority.'

Soviet prisoners were to be branded: 'The brand is to consist of an acute angle of about 45 degrees with a centimetre of length of side, pointing downwards on the left buttock at about a hand's width from the rectum.'

As Russia had not signed the Geneva Convention, the High Command said: 'Consequently we are not obliged to supply Soviet prisoners of war with food.'

The chief of prisoners of war in Poland was ordered to

construct open-air camps in which their captives were exposed to the elements. Orders were issued to poison prisoners who were unfit to work; political commissars were to be liquidated.

Soviet prosecutors read German reports showing that in one Lithuanian camp 13,936 prisoners had died from sickness between September 1941 and July 1942. More German records listed 130,000 prisoners of war who were tortured to death or shot in Stalag 350.

## *Understanding in our hearts*
Lengthy reports were read out on the use of civilian shields for the advancing German Army, the Einsatzkommandos, the murder of hostages, mass executions such as those at Babi Yar in the Ukraine (where 100,000 had been killed) and, to the discomfort of the Western delegations, the Katyn Forest. And the judges were handed samples of tanned skin and soap made from human bodies.

Birkett became impatient with this fresh catalogue of horrors and ceased taking notes, while Biddle raised 'a polite criticism of the slowness of the trial'. Judge Parker was disbelieving.

'They claimed today that the guards threw babies up and shot them in the camps,' he complained to an aide. 'You know no one would do that.'

Writing in the *Daily Herald*, journalist Maurice Fagence spoke of the Soviet prosecutor's voice droning on: 'He was speaking about the murder of millions of men, women and children. The court yawned .... We were thankful when the court rose and we filed to the tribunal cafeteria to sup tea and talk sweet nothings. Presently a little Russian captain entered. We saw him pay 1/6d for his snack and put down his tray. Suddenly he plunged his head into his hands and began to sob. "Oh mother, sweet mother, dear father, why did they kill you?" Then, with understanding in our hearts, we went back to court.'

## Atrocities in the USSR

The Soviets had a film of their own called *The Atrocities of the German Fascist Invaders in the USSR*. It was 45 minutes long and shocking even to those who had seen the American film earlier.

It showed a warehouse at Majdanek in which 800,000 pairs of shoes were stacked. There were piles of skulls, broken bodies and mutilated corpses – giant bone crushers going to work on 150,000 corpses in the Blagorschine Forest. One sequence showed naked women being driven towards mass graves, where they were forced to lie down and were shot by guards who smiled for the cameras. Other women were shown going through piles of stiff corpses, searching for their husbands and children.

Judge Parker was no longer sceptical. He retired to his bed for three days. After that, there were no further requests for the prosecution to speed up.

## Campaign of robbery

When the German Army invaded the Soviet Union in 1941, they were caught out in their summer uniforms by the onset of winter. The Soviet prosecutors quoted orders from the German Staff saying: 'It is urgently necessary that articles of clothing be acquired by means of forced levies on the population .... enforced by every means possible. It is necessary above all to confiscate woollen and leather gloves, coats, vests and scarves, padded vests and trousers, leather and felt boots, and puttees.' As a result hundreds of thousands of civilians froze to death.

The ideology behind the looting of the East came from former defendant Robert Ley, who said: 'It is our destiny to belong to a superior race. A lower race needs less room, less clothing, less food and less culture than a superior race.'

Orders were found in the area around Kursk and Orel that said: 'Property such as scales, sacks, grain, salt, kerosene, benzine, lamps, pots and pans, oilcloth, window blinds, curtains, rugs, phonographs and records must be turned in to the commandant's office. Anyone violating this order will be shot.'

The prosecutors went on: 'In the town of Istra, in the Moscow region, the invaders confiscated decorations for Christmas trees and toys. In the Shakhovskaya railway station they organized the "delivery" by the inhabitants of children's underwear, wall clocks and samovars. In districts still under the rule of the invaders, these searches are still going on; and the population, already reduced to the utmost poverty by the thefts which have been perpetrated continually since the first appearance of the German troops, is still being robbed ....

'The general character of the campaign of robbery planned by the Hitler Government, on which the German Command tried to base its plans for supplying its army and the districts in its rear, is indicated by the following facts: In 25 districts of the Tula region alone the invaders robbed Soviet citizens of 14,048 cows, 11,860 hogs, 28,459 sheep, 213,678 chickens, geese, and ducks, and destroyed 25,465 beehives.'

## *Wanton destruction*

Where they did not loot, they wantonly destroyed. The commander of the 98th Division ordered that 'available stocks of hay, straw, food supplies are to be burned. All stoves in houses should be put out of action so their further use can be made impossible.' This was a sentence of death to a Russian family.

On the estate of Leo Tolstoy, the Russian author's books

were used as fuel. When the officer in charge was told that there was plenty of firewood available, he said he preferred the light of Russian literature. Tchaikovsky's manuscripts were burned. Precious books were thrown out into the muddy streets of Kharkov for the wheels of trucks to grip. The tapestries were ripped from the walls of the Hradschin Castle in Prague, but little else was looted. It seemed that Slavic art was not to German taste and most of what the Nazis came across was destroyed.

When the German Army withdrew from a district it was to be razed. 'In order to carry out a complete destruction, all the houses shall be burned .... Structures of stone are to be blown up, particularly cellars,' one infantry colonel ordered. And preparations were to be made in secret. 'On the day designated particularly strict watch should be kept on inhabited localities so as not to allow any civilians to leave them.'

## *Murder and enslavement*

Jacob Gigoriev, a peasant from the Soviet District of Pskov near Leningrad, was called. He testified that Kusnezovo, the village in which he had lived, no longer existed. On 28 October 1943, 'German soldiers suddenly raided our village and started murdering the peaceful citizens, shooting them, chasing them into the houses.' Forty-seven villagers were killed. No defence counsel chose to cross-examine.

The question of slave labour was also addressed. A letter from a German private was read. He had seen women and children who worked 14 or more hours a day dropping from exhaustion then being whipped by the guards. There was an affidavit from a young woman taken from Kursk with her sister. They were pushed into a cattle truck with 50 or 60 others.

'In Lgov we had to get out and be examined,' she said.

## CHAPTER EIGHT

'In the presence of soldiers we were now compelled to undress quite naked and have our bodies examined. The nearer we got to Germany the fewer were the people left in the train ... at nearly every station the sick and those dying from hunger were thrown out.'

### *Genocide*

Soviet prosecutor Smirnov then turned his attention to the extermination of the Jews. Yiddish poet Abraham Sutzkever was called. He testified that about 80,000 Jews had lived in Vilnius before German occupation. In 1941, the Germans initiated a pogrom in Vilnius. At the end of the German occupation only 600 Jews had survived, with the remainder – approximately 79,400 – having been exterminated. No defence counsel chose to cross-examine.

His testimony was followed by that of Severina Schmaglevska, who had been interned in the Birkenau section of the Auschwitz concentration camp from October 1942 to January 1945. She said in Russian that children born in the camp were promptly taken from their mothers. If Jewish, they were put to death, often by hurling them alive into the furnaces of the crematorium. Non-Jewish children were put in a special block to be delivered to unknown destinations. No defence counsel elected to cross-examine.

At the end of the morning session, Dönitz's counsel Kranzbühler asked his client: 'Didn't anybody know anything about any of these things?' Dönitz shook his head. Overhearing, Göring said: 'Of course not. The higher you stand the less you see of what is going on below.' The defendants ate their lunch in silence that day.

### *'Road to heaven'*

Samuel Rajzman, an inmate of the Warsaw ghetto sent to Treblinka, testified that the German guards called the death camp the 'Road to heaven'. He said that an average of three transports totalling 60 car-loads each day arrived at Treblinka.

'Immediately after their arrival, the people had to leave the trains in five minutes and line up on the platform,' he said. 'All those who were driven from the cars were divided into groups – men, children and women, all separate. They were all forced to strip immediately, and this procedure continued under the lashes of the German guards' whips. Workers who were employed in this operation immediately picked up all the clothes and carried them away to barracks. Then the people were obliged to walk naked through the street to the gas chambers.'

It was called Himmelfahrtstrasse – literally, the 'street to heaven'. The whole process, for men, took eight to ten minutes. For women, it took 15 minutes, because their hair had to be cut off to stuff mattresses. Rajzman had been spared because of his language skills.

He told of the special treatment meted out to weak women and little children who did not have the strength to go into the gas chambers. They went to the so-called 'Lazarett'.

'This was part of a square which was closed in with a wooden fence,' he said. 'All women, aged persons, and sick children were driven there. At the gates of this "Lazarett", there was a large Red Cross flag. Menz, who specialized in the murder of all persons brought to this "Lazarett", would not let anybody else do this job. There might have been hundreds of persons who wanted to see and know what was in store for them, but he insisted on carrying out this work by himself.

'Here is just one example of what was the fate of the children there. A ten-year-old girl was brought to this building from the train with her two-year-old sister. When the elder girl saw that Menz had taken out a revolver to shoot her two-year-old sister, she threw herself upon him,

## CHAPTER EIGHT

crying out, and asking why he wanted to kill her. He did not kill the little sister; he threw her alive into the oven and then killed the elder sister.

'Another example: They brought an aged woman with her daughter to this building. The latter was in the last stage of pregnancy. She was brought to the "Lazarett", was put on a grass plot, and several Germans came to watch the delivery. This spectacle lasted two hours. When the child was born, Menz asked the grandmother – that is the mother of this woman – whom she preferred to see killed first. The grandmother begged to be killed. But, of course, they did the opposite; the newborn baby was killed first, then the child's mother and finally the grandmother.'

The station at Treblinka was dressed up to look like any other station. The barracks where the clothing was stored had signs reading 'restaurant', 'ticket office', 'telegraph', 'telephone' and so forth. There were even train schedules for the departure and the arrival of trains to and from Grodno, Suwalki, Vienna and Berlin.

Rajzman reckoned that 10–12,000 people were killed every day at Treblinka. There were plans to increase the number of ovens from ten to 25 to keep up with the output of the gas chambers.

He witnessed the arrival of his own mother, sister and two brothers. Friends going through the victims' clothes gave him a photograph they had found. It was of his wife and child. Again the defence declined to cross-examine.

A statement from Jacob Vernik, a carpenter from Warsaw who was also at Treblinka, was read.

'Awake or asleep I see terrible visions of thousands of people calling for help, begging for life and mercy,' it said. 'I have lost my family, I have myself led them to death; I have myself built the death chambers in which they were murdered. I am afraid of everything, I fear that everything

I have seen is written on my face. An old and broken life is a heavy burden, but I must carry on and live to tell the world what German crimes and barbarism I saw.'

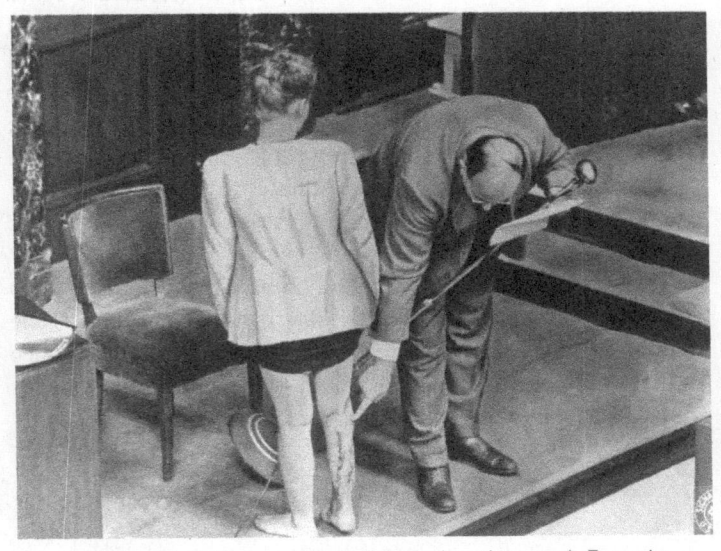

*A victim of medical experimentation takes the stand. Even the defendants found some of the evidence of what happened in the camps harrowing.*

### *'History will not be deceived'*

Four days were then given over to the arguments against Nazi organizations, led by Jackson. The case for the prosecution had lasted 73 days. Some 33 witnesses had been called and more than 2,000 documents presented. Many of the defendants had been condemned out of their own mouths.

Then, for the defendants at least, a miracle happened. Winston Churchill made his famous speech in Fulton, Missouri, saying: 'From Stettin in the Baltic to Trieste in

## CHAPTER EIGHT

the Adriatic, an iron curtain has descended across the Continent.' The enemy now, in Churchill's eyes at least, was the Soviet Union.

Speer described their 'tremendous excitement. Hess suddenly stopped playing the amnesiac and reminded us of how often he had predicted a great turning point that would put an end to the trial, rehabilitate all of us and restore us to our ranks and dignities. Göring, too, was beside himself; he repeatedly slapped his thighs with his palms and boomed: "History will not be deceived. The Führer and I always prophesied it. This coalition had to break up sooner or later."'

Hitler had always maintained that Nazi Germany was the great bulwark against Bolshevism. Until almost the end, he believed that it might be possible to forge an alliance with the Western Allies to defeat the Communist hordes marching from the east. As in many things, he was sadly deluded.

# Chapter Nine
## Opening for the Defence

Göring was particularly ebullient after Churchill's speech. He said: 'What did I tell you? Last summer I couldn't even hope to live till autumn. And now, I'll probably live through winter, summer, and spring and many times over. Mark my words. They'll be fighting among themselves before sentence can be pronounced on us.'

And, naturally, Göring was going to be the lead for the defence.

The first witness called by Stahmer, his defence counsel, was General Karl Bodenschatz, liaison officer between the Luftwaffe and Hitler's headquarters. He testified that, on Göring's instruction, he had helped perhaps ten to 20 Jews who had been arrested or were threatened with arrest and that Göring had opposed war against Britain and the Soviet Union.

It was noted that Bodenschatz was reading his testimony from a prepared statement. Jackson objected, but Lawrence allowed Bodenschatz to continue as he had been with Hitler in the Wolf's Lair on 20 July 1944 and had been injured in the bomb blast. According to Bodenschatz, Göring knew nothing about the attacks on Jews and their property on Kristallnacht – 9–10 November 1938. Nor was he aware of conditions in the concentration camps or the extermination of the Jews.

Jackson tore into Bodenschatz, making the point that two days after Kristallnacht Göring had promulgated the order fining Jews 1 billion Reichsmark, confiscated their insurance payments and passed a new decree excluding them from economic life.

When asked how he knew about a meeting he had said taken place, Bodenschatz said: 'Dr Stahmer told me so.' This produced laughter in the courtroom. Bodenschatz began to sweat profusely. Then he was asked about Göring's boast, early in the war, that his Luftwaffe would keep Germany safe from air attack. Göring was beside himself. A reporter from the *Evening Standard* noted: 'He gnashed his teeth and his eyes blazed with fury.'

## Milch and von Brauchitsch

Next came Secretary of State for the Air Ministry Erhard Milch, who maintained that Göring had built up the Luftwaffe for defensive purposes only; but he was forced to admit that, with a roughly equal number of fighters and bombers at the outbreak of war, it had been designed to support the army in the blitzkrieg form of warfare.

Milch was easy to undermine. He insisted that the foreign workers in Germany had been volunteers. However, he had been a member of the Central Planning Board and had been present at a meeting in which Sauckel had presented figures showing that only 200,000 out of 5 million were volunteers, and another in which Speer had said that slackers should be sent to concentration camps.

The minutes of the Central Planning Board also showed that he knew about the forced labour of prisoners of war – even that he found it 'amusing' that Russian prisoners of war were used to man guns. Records showed that he knew about the prosecution of an aggressive war, having been at a planning meeting on Poland on 23 March 1939, more than five months before the invasion had taken place. His correspondence with Himmler showed that he knew about experiments on prisoners in concentration camps investigating

## Opening for the Defence

the effects of low air pressure at high altitude and exposure. Milch left the stand, the *New York Times* said, 'a confused and wilted witness who had contributed as much to the prosecution case as he tried to detract from it'.

A subsequent military tribunal in Nuremberg sentenced him to life imprisonment. The sentence was later commuted and he was released in 1954.

Göring's adjutant, Bernd von Brauchitsch, admitted that his boss had transmitted Hitler's orders that Allied 'terror-fliers' should be lynched, but said he hoped they would not be put into practice. A former secretary of state in the Prussian State Ministry, he claimed that Germany had increased the efficiency of agriculture in the occupied territories and was, thus, entitled to a share of the surplus.

### *Kesselring*

Field Marshal Albert Kesselring made more of an impression, appearing in his Luftwaffe uniform. Jackson's cross-examination barely dented him. But Maxwell Fyfe confronted him with evidence that he had ordered the bombing of Rotterdam after negotiations for its surrender had begun. Then there were orders concerning partisans that Kesselring had given on 17 June 1944, when he was in command in Italy, which said: 'It is the duty of all troops and police in my command to adopt the severest measures .... Wherever there is evidence of considerable numbers of partisan groups, a proportion of the male population of the area will be arrested; and in the event of an act of violence being committed, these men will be shot.'

Maxwell Fyfe than read a UN War Crimes Commission report of what happened a week later:

> *Two German soldiers were killed and a third wounded in a fight with partisans in the village of Civitella.*

## CHAPTER NINE

*Hitler's chief strategist Field Marshal Albert Kesselring appeared for the defence at Nuremberg, but could not withstand the cross-examination of Maxwell Fyfe.*

*Fearing reprisals, the inhabitants evacuated the village, but when the Germans discovered this, punitive action was postponed. On June 29, when the local inhabitants were returning and were feeling secure once more, the Germans carried out a well-organized reprisal, combing the neighbourhood. Innocent inhabitants were often shot on sight. During that day 212 men, women and children in the immediate district were killed. Some of the dead women were found completely naked. In the course of investigations, a nominal roll of the dead has been compiled and is complete with the exception of a few names whose bodies could not be identified. Ages of the dead ranged from one year to eighty-four years. Approximately one*

> *hundred houses were destroyed by fire. Some of the victims were burned alive in their homes.*

'Now, witness, do you really think that military necessity commands the killing of babies of one and people of 84?' asked Maxwell Fyfe.

*The Times* said that Maxwell Fyfe's demolition of Kesselring was 'as masterly a piece of cross-examination as the court has heard'. Kesselring was sentenced to death by a British military tribunal sitting in Venice for ordering the execution of Italian hostages. His sentence was commuted and he was released in 1954.

### The Last Attempt

Göring's last witness was Swedish businessman Birger Dahlerus, a friend of Göring's first wife who had tried to broker peace in August 1939. Göring had arranged a meeting for him with Hitler. Why would a man hell-bent on war do such a thing? asked Stahmer.

Dahlerus had written a book about his efforts called *The Last Attempt*. Göring had read a copy in his cell. Maxwell Fyfe had a copy, too, and quoted liberally from it. In the book Dahlerus noted Göring's 'obsequious humility' towards Hitler, who ranted and screamed about 'planes, planes ... tanks, tanks' and 'exterminating the enemy'.

The book also detailed that Göring had demanded huge chunks of the Polish Corridor – the strip of land between East Prussia and the rest of Germany that gave Poland access to the Baltic – which he then called 'a magnanimous offer'. On 1 September, as the invasion of Poland was going ahead, Göring seemed to be 'in some crazy state of intoxication', said Dahlerus.

Not only did Dahlerus in his book and testimony damage Göring but he also accused Ribbentrop of trying to sabotage

## CHAPTER NINE

his plane and showed that, as foreign minister, he had done everything in his power to prevent the success of the negotiations.

As the cross-examination continued, Göring fumed, and pulled at the cord on his headphones until a guard took it out of his hands before it was ripped off. That evening, Ribbentrop turned to Kaltenbrunner and said: 'I don't know who to trust now.'

### Göring's testimony

The defence witnesses had done little to help Göring's cause. On 13 March 1946, it was his turn to take the stand in his own defence. Although be believed he was going to hang, Göring was determined to go down fighting. And he was going to be no pushover. He had always been physically

*On the stand Göring made an unapologetic defence of the Nazi regime, gibing at his accusers and winning plaudits from his co-defendants.*

## Opening for the Defence

imposing. But now he had been weaned off paracodeine and slimmed down by the prison diet, he was mentally agile and the documents presented in evidence against him were largely in German, which the prosecutors had to read in translation. And tales of his self-indulgence – his drug addiction, painted nails, made-up face and love of colourful uniforms – made him all too easy to underestimate.

He was nervous when he took the stand, but under the gentle questioning of Dr Stahmer he soon relaxed. Given the rift between the Soviets and the West following Churchill's Fulton speech, he was eager to emphasize that his disagreement with Hitler over the invasion of the Soviet Union was only over its timing.

He was also happy to help his co-defendants, especially over the charge of conspiracy. Only he was close enough to Hitler to have conspired with him, he maintained. He also gave them the shelter of the Führerprinzip – the principle that all decisions came from the leader, who had no time for cabinet meetings or the opinions of his generals.

His jibes at his accusers also struck home. Hitler had made himself head of state, head of the government and head of the armed forces, he said, 'following the example of the United States'. While Germany was accused of using Soviet resources for their own ends, they had not transported away the entire economy 'down to the last bolt and screw' as the Russians were then doing in the German territories they occupied. Criticism of Germany's need for living space did not sit well in the mouths of the Four Powers who 'call more than three-quarter of the globe their own'. And defending Germany against charges that it had broken the Hague conventions, he quoted Churchill saying: 'In the struggle for life and death there is in the end no legality.'

## CHAPTER NINE

### *Faith in their leaders*

Concentration camps had been established for 'protective custody'. Only military targets in Poland were bombed. In the Netherlands, the bombing had been intended to end the campaign as quickly as possible, thereby saving lives. Yugoslavia had been attacked because she was mobilizing. Leningrad was the only Russian city to suffer starvation – and that was because it was under siege. Otherwise the Germans had built up Russian agriculture and industry, not destroyed it.

He knew nothing about the lynching of 'terror-fliers', nor the summary execution of the prisoners of war from Stalag Luft III at Sagan after the 'Great Escape' – as he had been on leave at the time; the celebrated escapes by tunnelling from the Stalag Luft III camp near modern Zagan, Poland, were later dramatized in the films *The Great Escape* (1963) and *The Wooden Horse* (1950). The workers in the Luftwaffe's underground factories here were better off than those in the camps – 'given what is known now'. The Russian anti-aircraft gunners were volunteers. When it came to looting, the artworks he had taken had been deserted by their owners. He was protecting them from destruction, though perhaps 'my collector's passion got the better of me'. However, he had intended to pay for the objects he was wanted to keep. The others were to be sold to help French war victims.

After this bravura performance, the *Daily Express* said: 'The handshakes and plaudits, the bright eyes and smiles of his comrades in the dock, happier then they have been for months, are proof that he is winning them over to his last ditch stand of the Nazi regime in history.'

Göring had spent 12 hours in the witness box, almost uninterrupted by the bench. Birkett was horrified.

'It will have done much to restore German faith in their leaders,' he said.

### Opening for the Defence

## Cross-examination

Jackson opened the cross-examination on 18 March, after Göring had had the weekend to recuperate. The questions began with the early history of Nazism. Jackson sought to show that the crimes the Nazis committed were implicit in the origins of the party. But this approach gave Göring an opportunity to warm up.

Soon he was parrying every question. Instead of giving the 'yes' or 'no' answers Jackson required, he seized the opportunity to make long-winded speeches of exculpation. When Jackson appealed to judges to impose some limits on the witness, they said they wanted to hear what Göring had to say.

Jackson said that, according to Berlin SA leader Karl Ernst, Göring and Goebbels had provided the liquid phosphorus and petroleum for the attempt to burn down the Reichstag on 27 February 1933, which allowed Hitler to seize dictatorial powers. Göring said that Ernst had been shot on 30 June 1934, because together with Röhm he had planned to overthrow the government and had plotted against the Führer. Besides, the accusation of Göring's complicity came from the foreign press.

'From the artistic point of view I did not at all regret that the assembly chamber was burned; I hoped to build a better one,' he said. What he did regret was that the parliament had to meet in the Kroll Opera House instead. 'The opera seemed to me much more important than the Reichstag.'

At the end of the first day of cross-examination it was clear who was winning. One American reporter said: 'Jackson has been saved by the gong.'

## Mistranslation

The second day went no better. When Jackson produced a document referring to 'preparation for the liberation of the

## CHAPTER NINE

Rhine' nine months earlier than Göring had claimed, Göring said the document had been mistranslated. It read 'preparation for the *clearing* of the Rhine' – the river, not the Rhineland – and referred only to clearing the Rhine of civilian traffic in the event of war. Nevertheless, Jackson insisted, plans for the armed occupation of the Rhineland were kept secret.

'I do not think I can recall reading beforehand the publication of the mobilization preparations of the United States,' Göring jibed.

Jackson complained of Göring's 'arrogant and contemptuous attitude toward the tribunal which is giving him the trial which he never gave a living soul'.

Lawrence ruled that Göring's remark about the mobilization of the United States was irrelevant, but gave Jackson little more assistance and Göring continued to run rings around him.

Jackson struck back with a litany of crude anti-Semitic remarks reputedly made by Göring that dented his image as a suave and sophisticated man. And documents showing Göring's complicity in the Holocaust could not be refuted no matter how much Göring cavilled about mistranslations.

Göring had no pat answers when the records of his stolen art treasures were introduced – nor when details of the stripping of Russian resources were presented. But then Jackson faltered. He turned his attention to the comparatively trivial matter of the destruction of the American ambassador's house in Warsaw. Seeking to prove that it had been deliberately targeted by the Luftwaffe, he produced what he said were aerial photographs. Göring had been a pilot in the First World War and knew a great deal about aerial photography. The picture, he demonstrated, had been taken from the top of a church steeple. On the back there was no date or departmental stamp. Then he said, almost contemptuously: 'However, let

**Opening for the Defence**

us assume that they were taken by the Luftwaffe, so that further questions will be facilitated.'

Jackson was floored.

## *British onslaught*

Cross-examination then passed to the British, but most of the prosecution's ammunition had been spent. The tribunal had already ruled that ground already covered could not be touched on again. However, Maxwell Fyfe was a skilled trial lawyer. He showed that Göring was not on leave when the Great Escape prisoners had been shot. As time was short that day, he went on to the Luftwaffe policy of sending all escapers, except British and Americans, to be killed at Mauthausen. Göring was rattled.

The following morning, Maxwell Fyfe went back to the Stalag Luft III killings. Remorselessly, he established Göring's involvement. When Göring sought to dissemble, Maxwell Fyfe cut him short.

At first Göring said that Ribbentrop had known nothing about the negotiations with Dahlerus, then that he had resented them. Which was it?

Göring could do no more than bluster over his prior knowledge of the invasion of Poland, the deliberate violation of the neutrality of Belgium and the Netherlands and the attack on Yugoslavia.

A barrage of documents about Auschwitz and the use of forced labour showed that Göring knew about it or was guilty of criminal negligence over crimes committed in his name. And he was also implicated in atrocities against partisans.

The *Daily Telegraph* said his face became 'strained and congested'. *The Times* said: 'Göring's denials sounded far less plausible than at any time ... he ever sounded less sure of himself.'

## CHAPTER NINE

### *Unshakeable loyalty*

Göring's only defence was his unshakeable loyalty to Hitler, insisting that the Führer had known nothing about the Holocaust. His policy was 'emigration not liquidation'. Himmler had kept the death camps secret, Göring said. In response, Maxwell Fyfe read from the record of a discussion between Hitler and the Regent of Hungary, Admiral Horthy. In it, Hitler said: 'In Poland, this state of affairs had been fundamentally cleared up. If the Jews there did not want to work, they were shot. If they could not work, they had to perish. They had to be treated like tuberculosis bacilli, with which a healthy body may become infected. This was not cruel – if one remembers that even innocent creatures of nature, such as hares and deer, have to be killed so that no harm is caused by them.'

When Horthy asked what he should do with the Jews in Hungary, Hitler replied: 'The Reich minister for foreign affairs declared that the Jews should be exterminated, or taken to concentration camps. There was no other possibility.'

Göring said he did not know about this. So Maxwell Fyfe read another document in which Göring was told: 'There are only a few Jews left alive. Tens of thousands have been disposed of ... '

Göring rallied slightly during Rudenko's cross-examination, but left the witness stand – according to the *New York Times* – 'with a wilted and bedraggled air'.

## Chapter Ten
# Hitler's Henchmen

Hess decided not to take the witness stand in his own defence. He told Gilbert that he did not want to suffer the embarrassment of not being able to answer the prosecution questions, though his counsel, Dr Alfred Seidl, said it was because he did not recognize the jurisdiction of the court, other than in the matter of war crimes. As he had been in

*Rudolf Hess admitted his role in the Nazi Party and accepted responsibility for his actions, while challenging the tribunal's right to judge their legality.*

## CHAPTER TEN

British custody since May 1941, there was little for him to answer for on that score. Again the tribunal pointed out that the Charter prohibited any dispute over its authority.

Seidl tried to introduce a collection of press cuttings and speeches criticizing the Versailles Treaty. Biddle asked Seidl if the provisions of the treaty – no matter how unjust they were said to be – and their infraction by others could justify the war and the horrors perpetrated in it. When Seidl failed to make a cogent argument to that effect the evidence was ruled inadmissible.

His attempt to cause discord by introducing in evidence the secret protocol to the Molotov-Ribbentrop Pact that carved up Poland between Germany and the Soviet Union was also thwarted.

An affidavit from Hess's former secretary asserted her belief that Hess had flown to Britain with the sole desire of promoting peace.

Seidl then called Ernst Bohle, who had worked for Hess as head of the Auslands-Organization – the Nazi Party's foreign wing. He claimed that Germans living abroad had never been ordered to commit any illegal act in their country of residence either by Hitler or Hess. It was easy to show that the organization had provided the Nazi regime with military intelligence.

Hess was prepared to admit his role in the Nazi Party and accept responsibility for his acts as part of the government – while challenging the tribunal's right to judge their legality. Maxwell Fyfe decided to list them and get Seidl to confirm or deny the accuracy of his account. Hess had joined the embryonic Nazi Party in 1920 and had introduced the concept of *lebensraum* – 'living space', to be taken from the Slavic people in the east. In Landsberg prison he had taken dictation for Hitler's autobiographical manifesto *Mein Kampf* and edited it. Photographs were introduced to show that Hess was Hitler's constant companion, and was made Deputy Führer in 1933. Two years later, he signed the Nuremberg Laws for Blood and Honour, formalizing the persecution of the Jews, and the decree for compulsory military service, significantly contributing to preparations for war. He had also signed laws incorporating Austria, Danzig and Poland into the Reich. And when he flew to Britain, he already knew that preparations were being made for an attack on the Soviet Union. The prosecution contended that Hess had flown to Britain in an effort to secure peace so that Germany would have to fight on one front only.

Those arguments covered conspiracy and waging an aggressive war. The evidence against Hess for war crimes and crimes against humanity was thinner. He had made a statement about sending Waffen-SS units into the eastern territories because of their 'intensive National Socialist training' – implying they would be used for pogroms. There was also a complaint from the Ministry of Justice in 1941 over Hess urging the corporal punishment of Poles.

The case for the defence lasted barely a day. Hess spent much of his time making comments to his fellow defendants and was twice seized with inexplicable laughter.

## *Ribbentrop*

Dr Martin Horn, Ribbentrop's counsel, had a more formidable task. While minutes of one meeting showed that Ribbentrop was against the lynching of enemy pilots who had attacked civilians, elsewhere he suggested that all captured airmen should suffer instant execution. Documents showed that he had urged foreign governments to exterminate Jews and that his ministry had looted artwork and colluded in the deportation of foreign workers to Germany.

When his turn came on 25 March, Ribbentrop announced that he was too ill to attend. The prison doctor could find

## CHAPTER TEN

nothing wrong with him and he was compelled to attend the following day.

*Joachim von Ribbentrop, ambassador to the Court of St James in 1937, on his way to present his diplomatic credentials to George VI.*

Horn began by trying to enter into evidence a huge number of documents, many of which had not been translated, were copies or had no proof of authenticity. The tribunal ruled more than half of them inadmissible.

The first witness for the defence was Baron Gustav Steengracht von Moyland, who had been Ribbentrop's adjutant before being promoted to State Secretary at the Foreign Ministry in 1943. Steengracht said: 'The foreign policy, not only on its basic lines, but also usually down to the most minute details, was determined by Hitler himself. Ribbentrop frequently stated that the Führer needed no foreign minister .'

Himmler, Goebbels, Bormann and Göring had a certain

influence; Ribbentrop had none. Nevertheless he had somehow managed to check Hitler's excesses and stayed on in office to prevent someone worse taking over. Steengracht read his testimony from a prepared sheet and was admonished for doing so.

## Admiration and veneration

Then Ribbentrop's secretary Margarete Blank was called. She managed to undermine much of Steengracht's testimony, saying: 'Herr von Ribbentrop always showed the greatest admiration and veneration for Adolf Hitler. To enjoy the Führer's confidence, to justify it by his conduct and work was his chief aim.'

The final witness for Ribbentrop's defence was his interpreter. Questioned by Maxwell Fyfe, he confirmed what he had said in his affidavit: 'The general objectives of the Nazi leadership were apparent from the start, namely, the domination of the European Continent, to be achieved, first, by the incorporation of all German-speaking groups in the Reich, and secondly, by territorial expansion under the slogan of "Lebensraum".'

What's more, when Hitler outlined these aims at a confrence which most of the defendants attended, no one had objected.

## Sunken and pallid

As Ribbentrop took his place in the witness box, according to the *Daily Telegraph*, 'his face was drawn, his cheeks were sunken and pallid .... His gait was halting as he walked to the witness stand clutching a file of papers.'

He began reading a prepared statement in a lifeless voice, rambling on about the iniquities of the Versailles Treaty and the horrors of Germany's economic collapse. Then came his first meeting with Hitler in 1932 where he thought:

## CHAPTER TEN

'This man, if anyone, would save Germany from these great difficulties and that distress.'

The following morning, Lawrence reminded the court that both the Versailles Treaty and the history of the Nazi Party had already been dealt with. Further discussion of these matters was inadmissible. Nevertheless, Ribbentrop continued a meandering diatribe on how the other nations had ganged up on Germany. The *Daily Telegraph* called it 'a nebulous apologia which only narrowly escaped the stigma of cowardice'. To *The Times*, Ribbentrop's waffle explained why it was impossible to have any diplomatic dealing with Germany before the war. His fellow defendants, who had expected some robust defence of German foreign policy, were in despair.

Ribbentrop and Göring even had a row about it in the dock until they were called to order. Göring then copied Hess and started reading a book. But Andrus would not have it, telling him to stop reading as it was an insult to the tribunal.

### 'We want war'

Maxwell Fyfe then went in for the kill with the minutes of meetings and other documents. Ribbentrop had maintained in his testimony that he did not want war, but when Italian foreign minister Count Gian Galeazzo Ciano asked him in 1939 whether Germany wanted the Polish Corridor or Danzig, he replied: 'Not any more; we want war.' Then when the war began he said he was glad about the turn of events because it would be a good thing if the conflict was finished in the lifetime of the Führer.

When Ribbentrop dismissed his discussions with Ciano as 'nothing but diplomatic talk', Maxwell Fyfe asked: 'Don't you think there is any requirement to tell the truth in a political conversation?'

Ribbentrop claimed to have been only an honorary

member of the SS, because as an ambassador and later as foreign minister he was considered by Hitler to warrant a uniform and some rank. But evidence was entered showing that he had applied to join the SS – and was accepted – three years before he became an ambassador. He got a ring and a dagger as a member of the Death's Head Division.

It had been established that Ribbentrop had done very well out of becoming a Nazi and had no fewer than six houses. The one at Fuschl was near the group of camps at Mauthausen, shown on a map in the courtroom. There were 33 separate units there, housing 100,000 people. Ribbentrop must have flown over it several times when he went to stay. He could hardly maintain that he knew nothing about concentration camps.

Maxwell Fyfe went on to the harsh treatment of partisans. Ribbentrop denied involvement in such things, but the documents recorded him saying 'partisan gangs had to be exterminated, including men, women, and children' and urging 'merciless action' in Norway, Italy and Greece. After Maxwell Fyfe's cross-examination Ribbentrop collapsed and had to be helped back to his cell.

When it was the turn of Edgar Faure, French counsel for the prosecution, to conduct the cross-examination, he reminded Ribbentrop of the testimony Maxwell Fyfe had read to Göring, where Hitler told Horthy: 'The Reich minister for foreign affairs' – that is, Ribbentrop – 'declared that the Jews should be exterminated, or taken to concentration camps. There was no other possibility.'

All Ribbentrop could say was that he had not used those words.

## *Keitel*

Keitel saw himself as a Prussian officer, though Göring described him as having 'a sergeant's mind inside a field

## CHAPTER TEN

marshal's body'. A lifelong military man, he believed a soldier's job was to obey. His colleagues called him 'Lackeitel' – the lackey. Others knew him as 'Nickesef' – a toy donkey with a constantly nodding head. Two shorthand writers who attended military conferences said they never bothered to write down Keitel's first sentence – it was always identical to Hitler's last.

Throughout the trial, he was immaculately turned out for the occasion and made no apologies for his actions. The Wehrmacht and the soldier were tools of the politicians, he said: 'they are not qualified in my opinion to decide or to judge whether these military operations did or did not constitute a war of aggression.'

Though orders sent out bore Keitel's signature, they were in fact Hitler's orders. These included plans of invasion, orders to seize food and loot in occupied areas, to seize and execute hostages, to lynch commandos and commissars, to deport workers to Germany as slave labour and to maltreat prisoners of war – along with the notorious *Nacht und Nebel* decree. He disapproved and his conscience was clear.

'The traditional training and concept of duty of the German officers, which taught unquestioning obedience to superiors who bore responsibility, led to an attitude – regrettable in retrospect – which caused them to shrink from rebelling against these orders and these methods even when they recognized their illegality and inwardly refuted them,' he said.

Everything was Hitler's fault because he 'abused his authority ... in an irresponsible way in respect to use'.

There was no opportunity to question an order. At a military conference, 'the Führer arrived, spoke and went out. No one in such a situation could have found an opening to say anything.'

But still Keitel was enamoured of Hitler. He was self-taught in military matters and, consequently, 'a genius'.

'I was the pupil not the master,' said Keitel.

When Canaris protested about the inhuman treatment of Russian prisoners of war, Keitel wrote: 'These objections arise from the military conception of chivalrous warfare. We are dealing here with the destruction of an ideology and I therefore approve such measures and I sanction them.'

In his *Nacht und Nebel* Decree, he said: 'Effective and lasting intimidation can only be achieved whether by capital punishment or by means which leave the relatives and the population in the dark about the fate of the culprit. Deportation to Germany serves this purpose.'

And he issued an order to suppress insurrection in the Occupied Eastern Territories in 1941, saying: 'In order to nip in the bud any conspiracy, the strongest measures should be taken at the first sign of trouble in order to maintain the authority of the occupying power and to prevent the conspiracy from spreading ... one must bear in mind that in the countries affected human life has absolutely no value and that a deterrent effect can be achieved only through the application of extraordinarily harsh measures.'

The document demanded the death penalty of 50 or 100 communists for every one German soldier killed. Keitel insisted that he had originally written five to ten, but Hitler had changed it, and the German document said: '... in the countries affected human life frequently has no value ... '

Only Maxwell Fyfe made any dent in Keitel's haughty demeanour. When Keitel talked of handing a prisoner over to the SD, he implied that it was like putting the prisoner into police custody. Maxwell Fyfe responded: 'You have been at this trial too long to think that handing people over to the SD means police custody. It means concentration camps and a gas chamber, does it not?'

## CHAPTER TEN

*Field Marshal Wilhelm Keitel speaking during the trials. He described himself as a pupil to Hitler's master.*

When Keitel proffered a kind of apology for his orders to punish families of Frenchmen found fighting alongside the Russians, and expressed regret that these relatives had been held responsible for 'the misdeeds of their sons', Maxwell Fyfe interjected: 'If you think that is a misdeed, it is not worth our discussing it further.'

The *New York Times* reported that Keitel began to stammer, and was forced to agree that his orders were cruel and despicable. As further blows rained down, he was seen 'leaning back groggily in his chair, groping for words'.

Maxwell Fyfe aimed one last savage kick at his Prussian pride.

'You were a Field Marshal, standing in the boots of Blücher, Gneisenau and Moltke.' These were Keitel's military heroes. 'How did you tolerate all these young men being murdered, one after another without making any protest?'

All Keitel could say was that he could add nothing to the statement he had made earlier. His testimony had done nothing to rebut the charges made against him. Witnesses called in his defence were little help, either. Dr Hans Lammers, chief of the Reich Chancellery from 1933 to 1945, said that, in his opinion, no programme for the extermination of Jews had ever been set up, though it was possible that some had been shot in some town or other in wartime. In a subsequent trial, he was sentenced to 20 years, but was released in 1951.

Keitel tried to drop two further defence witnesses – General Adolf Westhoff, chief of prisoners of war, and Max Wielen, the SS chief of police in Bresau. But the tribunal called them to question them on affidavits they had given on the Stalag Luft III murders. Their testimony further implicated Göring and Keitel. To the prosecution's frustration, the case against Keitel had taken seven days.

## Chapter Eleven
# Architects of the Holocaust

Although Hitler, Himmler and Eichmann were not at Nuremberg, a number of the principal architects of the Holocaust were on hand.

Kaltenbrunner was every inch a Nazi thug, but as he took the stand he appeared pale and nervous. Along with a massive list of charges against him personally as head of the RSHA, he was also to be tried as a representative of the Gestapo. He denied none of the crimes of which the RSHA and the Gestapo – and the SD under its control – were accused. He just maintained that he had nothing to do with them. Himmler, he said, had simply bypassed him.

Kaltenbrunner was cross-examined by American prosecutor Colonel John Amen, who presented damning testimony. First came the orders Kaltenbrunner had issued for British and American commandos to be shot, for SD members to be conscripted into the Einsatzkommandos, for anti-Jewish measures to be begun in Denmark, for Hungarian Jews to be worked to death and for 65,000 prisoners to be worked to death in Mauthausen. Kaltenbrunner denied everything. The signatures were facsimiles, the documents forged.

The only camp he had seen was Mauthausen – and it was a quarry, providing stone for the pavements of Vienna. The first he had heard of Auschwitz was in 1943; Himmler had told him it was an armaments factory. He never saw a gas chamber and had never heard of any policy to exterminate Jews – though minutes earlier he had claimed to have stopped the extermination.

Affidavits said that he visited Mauthausen three times. Inspecting the facilities, he 'went laughing into the gas chamber. Then the people were brought from the bunker to be executed, and then all three kinds of executions: hanging, shooting in the back of the neck and gassing, were demonstrated'.

'Not a single word of these statements is true,' said Kaltenbrunner.

He later complained: 'For a whole year I have had to submit to this insult of being called a liar.'

### *Höss*

Kaltenbrunner's chief witness for the defence was Rudolf Höss, the commandant of Auschwitz. He admitted to killing more than 2 million men, women and children, and took a certain pride in his work: Auschwitz was much more efficient than Treblinka, for example; Treblinka's gas chambers only accommodated 200 at a time, while at Auschwitz they had built their gas chambers to accommodate 2,000; and the Zyklon B they used at Auschwitz was much better than Treblinka's carbon monoxide gas.

Colonel Amen read parts of Höss's affidavit:

*It took from three to fifteen minutes to kill the people in the death chamber, depending upon climatic conditions. We knew when the people were dead because their screaming stopped. We usually waited about one half hour before we opened the doors and removed the bodies. After the bodies were removed our special Kommandos took off the rings and extracted the gold from the teeth of the corpses.*

'Is that true and correct, witness?' he asked.

## CHAPTER ELEVEN

*The gates of Auschwitz, one of the many extermination camps where the poison Zyklon B was used in a deliberate programme of mass murder.*

Höss said 'Yes' and Amen continued:

*Children of tender years were invariably exterminated since by reason of their youth they were unable to work. Still another improvement we made over Treblinka was that at Treblinka the victims almost always knew that they were to be exterminated and at Auschwitz we endeavoured to fool the victims into thinking that they were to go through a delousing process. Of course, frequently they realized our true intentions and we sometimes had riots and difficulties due to that fact. Very frequently women would hide their children under their clothes, but of course when we found them we would send the children in to be exterminated. We were required to carry out these exterminations in secrecy but of course the foul and nauseating stench from the continuous burning of bodies permeated the entire area and all of the people living in the surrounding communities knew that exterminations were going on at Auschwitz.*

'Is that all true and correct, witness?'

Höss said, 'Yes.' He was equally frank about the medical experiments that were carried out. This shocking testimony was received in silence. Over lunch the defendants were also silent, though Göring and Dönitz said that Höss must be from south Germany: no Prussian could have done such things.

In Kaltenbrunner's defence, Kaufmann, his counsel, pointed out that 'orders for protective custody, commitments, punishments, and special executions were signed by Kaltenbrunner or Müller, Chief of the Gestapo, as Kaltenbrunner's deputy.'

'I read only a few decrees signed by Kaltenbrunner; most of them were signed by Müller,' said Höss. 'All mass executions through gassing took place under the direct order, supervision and responsibility of RSHA. I received all orders for carrying out these mass executions directly from RSHA.'

It was easy for Amen to get Höss to admit that Müller was simply signing the orders as the representative of Kaltenbrunner, who was head of the RSHA.

At his trial in Warsaw, Höss was accused of murdering 3.5 million people. He protested: 'No, only two and a half – the rest died from disease and starvation.' He was hanged.

### *Rosenberg*

Jackson was furious when Rosenberg requested copies of documents, some 25,000 sheets in all. Paper, Jackson pointed out, was 'a scarce commodity today'. His counsel also asked for 260 extra copies of Rosenberg's book of documents to be printed for the press.

'The United States cannot be acting as press agent for the distribution of anti-Semitic literature,' Jackson protested.

While Rosenberg was one of the chief theoreticians of anti-Semitism, the charges against him focused on his time as minister for the Occupied Eastern Territories. Under cross-examination, Dodd confronted him with his own order that 'all inhabitants of the Occupied Eastern Territories are subject to the public liability for compulsory work.'

Then there was a speech he had delivered in 1941, in which he said: 'The job of feeding the German people stands this year, without doubt, at the top of the list of Germany's claims on the East .... We see absolutely no reason for any obligation on our part to feed also the Russian people with the products of that surplus-territory. We know that this is a harsh necessity, beyond feelings. A very extensive evacuation will be necessary, without any doubt, and it is sure that the future will hold very hard years in store for the Russians.'

Rosenberg pointed out that Russia had not signed the Geneva Convention and argued that the Hague conventions did not apply to the Soviet Union since it was 'considered dissolved'.

As Rosenberg had no real defence against the charges against him, he was allowed a little latitude.

'For hours he maundered on,' the *Manchester Guardian* reported. 'It was no more possible to grasp what he was saying than to seize a handful of cloud. Those who could went to get coffee or took an early lunch; others such as guards and messengers had to fall asleep.'

## Hans Frank

The 42 volumes of Frank's diary were enough to hang him. A former counsellor for Hitler, he was a slick operator in the courtroom. Asked by Seidl, his counsel: 'Did you ever participate in the annihilation of Jews?' He replied: 'I say "yes"; and the reason why I say "yes" is because, having lived through the five months of this trial, and particularly after having heard the testimony of the witness Höss, my conscience does not allow me to throw the responsibility solely on these minor people. I myself have never installed an extermination camp for Jews, or promoted the existence of such camps; but if Adolf Hitler personally has laid that dreadful responsibility on his people, then it is mine, too, for we have fought against Jewry for years; and we have indulged in the most horrible utterances. My own diary bears witness against me. Therefore, it is no more than my duty to answer your question in this connection with "yes". A thousand years will pass and still this guilt of Germany will not have been erased.'

His admission of guilt won him no friends in the dock, nor were the court swayed by this semblance of contrition.

## Wilhelm Frick

As minister of the interior from 1933 to 1943, Frick put in

## CHAPTER ELEVEN

place much of the apparatus of repression and went on to become 'protector' of Bohemia and Moravia. But although he was a lawyer, he declined to go in the witness box to defend himself. The suspicion was that he wanted to avoid questions about stolen money that he had hidden away for his wife and children.

Frick's counsel, Dr Otto Pannenberg, called Hans Bernd Gisevius, a former peacetime Gestapo officer who was sacked and had compiled dossiers of others' crimes. With the help of Canaris, he had escaped into Switzerland. He was also going to be a witness for Schacht.

Gisevius's contribution to Frick's defence was to say that he was 'a minister with no personal executive power'. Himmler overrode him; he had no access to Hitler and no influence over him. However, Frick had signed the decree legitimizing the murder of Röhm and the others on the 'Night of the Long Knives'. He was also in charge of the running of the concentration camps and was fully informed of the abuses that went on there.

With Gisevius on the stand, Jackson was free to cross-examine him about the other defendants: Ribbentrop, Jodl and Funk had more influence over Hitler than they let on; Neurath and Papen were fully aware of the activities of the Gestapo, while Keitl knew about the atrocities carried out by the Wehrmacht and the SS, the use of slave labour and the extermination of the Jews.

But, according to Gisevius, Göring was the biggest crook of all. Not only had Göring planned the Reichstag fire, he had arranged the murder of one of the perpetrators who had spoken to a magistrate when he had not been paid. What's more, Göring – along with Himmler and Hitler – had drawn up the list of those to be murdered during the Röhm purge, another name for the 'Night of the Long Knives'. Göring was so angry that, at the end of the session, he stood up in the dock

*Hitler's minister of the interior Wilhelm Frick in his cell at Nuremberg. Although he was a lawyer, he refused to take the stand to defend himself.*

haranguing all and sundry until he was manhandled away, to the lift.

### Streicher

The case against Streicher was weak. Although the anti-Semitism stirred up by his newspaper *Der Stürmer* had led to the Holocaust, he had killed no one. He had fallen from favour in 1938. In 1940 he had been stripped of office and retired to private life. But instead of leaving his counsel to argue that there was no case to answer, he insisted on taking the stand.

He began with an attack on his own counsel, Dr Hanns Marx, saying that he had been intimidated by the communist press. He then alleged that he had been kept naked in his cell, though Fritzsche had fashioned a pair of shorts for him to prevent him doing his morning exercises nude. He refused to wear them. He also claimed he had been made to 'kiss a negro's feet' and, when he had asked for a drink of water, had been made to drink from a latrine.

'These are the sort of things the Gestapo has been blamed for,' he said.

Then he began a rant about how the Jews had seized power in Germany in 1918. He had begun his own movement in Franconia but, three years later, when he saw Hitler speak in Munich 'drenched in perspiration, radiant', he handed it over, allowing the Nazi Party to expand outside Bavaria. Various allegations that had been made against him for rape and indecent behaviour were dismissed.

Streicher admitted organizing a boycott of Jewish businesses and claimed to have contributed indirectly to the Nuremberg race laws. On Kristallnacht, the main synagogue in Nuremburg had been burned down. He justified this on architectural grounds and submitted a photograph in evidence. He even gave a diatribe on the subject of Jews being responsible for ritual murder.

### 'A statement of fact'

None of the other defence counsels wished to cross-examine Streicher. The task fell to Lieutenant Colonel J.M.G. Griffith-Jones. He did not even look at Streicher, who continued his anti-Semitic rants. In 1943 Streicher had referred to Hitler's promise to 'free the world from its Jewish

## Architects of the Holocaust

tormentors', writing: 'How wonderful it is to know that this great man and leader is following up this promise with practical action.' Yet he denied knowing of any organized killing of Jews. He claimed to have been a subscriber to the Swiss publication *Israelitisches Wochenblatt* ('Israeli Weekly'), but could not recall any of the articles it carried about the dispossession and murder of Jews. Nevertheless in the press he continued to demand the 'annihilation' of the Jews. In *Der Stürmer* he referred to Jews as 'a nation of bloodsuckers and extortionists'.

Asked, 'Do you think that's preaching racial hatred?' he answered: 'No. It is not preaching racial hatred. It is just a statement of fact.'

There were arguments over what he meant when he used the word *vernichtet* – 'annihilate'.

Griffith-Jones read another extract from *Der Stürmer*: 'A punitive expedition must come against the Jews in Russia. A punitive expedition which will provide the same fate for them that every murderer and criminal must expect. Death sentence and execution. The Jews in Russia must be killed. They must be exterminated root and branch.'

Streicher denied writing this. But he was the editor of the newspaper and was forced to take responsibility for printing it.

Maxwell Fyfe decided that it would be best not to cross-examine Streicher's witnesses, rather treat them with disdain. In the hands of Dr Marx, they did more harm than good anyway. One of them was Streicher's wife, who testified that her husband had spent the war on his farm, editing the newspaper, and had no contact with Hitler. She was an attractive blonde woman, twenty years his junior. As she left the stand, Jodl remarked: 'Wondrous are the ways of love.' Lawrence ruled that Streicher's vast collection of pornography was no business of the tribunal.

## Chapter Twelve
# The Money Men

In the witness box, banker Hjalmar Schacht sought to justify his early support for the Nazi Party, saying he could see nothing criminal in its programme. But of *Mein Kampf* he said: 'It is a book written in the worst kind of German, propaganda of a man who was strongly interested in politics, not to say a fanatical, half-educated man, which to me Hitler has always been.'

Hitler, he said, 'was a mass psychologist of really diabolical genius ... He was a man of unbending energy, of a willpower which overcame all obstacles, and in my estimate only those two characteristics – mass psychology and his energy and willpower – explain that Hitler was able to rally up to 40 per cent, and later almost 50 per cent, of the German people behind him.'

Schacht said he had stayed in the government because 'I considered it my duty to put myself at the disposal of my people and my country for their good.' However, he criticized Hitler over the 'Night of the Long Knives': 'At that time I had told Hitler, "How could you have these people just simply killed off? Under all circumstances there should have been at least a summary trial of some sort." Hitler swallowed these remarks and merely mumbled something about "revolutionary necessity", but he did not really contradict me.'

He went on with a litany of criticism of Hitler:

'He promised equal rights for all citizens, but his adherents, regardless of their capabilities, enjoyed privileges before all other citizens. He promised to put the Jews under the same protection which foreigners enjoyed, yet he deprived them of every legal protection. He had promised to fight against political lies, but together with his minister, Goebbels, he cultivated nothing but political lies and political fraud. He promised the German people to maintain the principles of positive Christianity yet he tolerated and sponsored measures by which institutions of the Church were abused, reviled and damaged. Also, in the foreign political field he always spoke against a war on two fronts – and then later undertook it himself. He despised and disregarded all laws of the Weimar Republic, to which he had taken the oath when he became chancellor. He mobilized the Gestapo against personal liberty. He gagged and bound all free exchange of ideas and information. He pardoned criminals and enlisted them in his service. He did everything to break his promises. He lied to and deceived the world, Germany and me.'

Schacht distanced himself from the other defendants. Some he did not know. Others he had not seen since 1938.

'Most of the leaders of the Hitler Party were not exactly ideal types of the Nordic race,' he said. 'Only one thing ... did most of the leaders of the Party have in common with the old Teutons – and that was drinking; excessive drinking was a main part of the Nazi ideology.'

Gisevius supported much of what Schacht had to say. Schacht had only supported rearmament for self-defence. In 1935, Gisevius had found Gestapo bugging devices in Schacht's flat. Schacht had joined Gisevius on two secret trips to Switzerland to warn the British of Hitler's intention to invade Poland.

'He undoubtedly entered the Hitler regime for patriotic reasons,' he said, 'and I would like to testify here that the moment his disappointment became obvious he decided for the same patriotic reasons to join the opposition.'

# CHAPTER TWELVE

*Though Banker Hjalmar Schacht (third from right) had been arrested after the 20 July plot, he went on trial for helping Hitler in his rise to power.*

### Impressive witness

The *New York Times* said that Schacht was 'an impressive witness'. He was to be cross-examined by Jackson, who was judged to have done poorly against Göring and was seeking to redeem himself.

To establish the conspiracy, Jackson presented a series of photographs of Schacht with prominent Nazi figures. But there were no dates on the photographs and Schacht said

## The Money Men

if Jackson presented pictures of him with other acquaintances there would be ten times as many.

Schacht had claimed not to have been a member of the Nazi Party. However, Jackson pointed out that he often wore the Nazi Party's golden swastika.

'It was very convenient on railroad journeys, when ordering a car, etcetera,' said Schacht.

However, Schacht was forced to admit that he had contributed 1,000 Reichsmarks a year to the Nazi Party from 1937 to 1942 and had branded as traitors those who patronized Jewish shops.

The other defendants enjoyed this. Göring was overheard telling Hess: 'Put on your headphones. This is going to be good.'

But Göring did not always like what he heard. Questioning Schacht about his disagreement with Göring, which Schacht maintained was about rearmament, Jackson read from Schacht's pre-trial interrogation:

*Whereas I have called Hitler an amoral type of person, I can regard Göring only as immoral and criminal. Endowed by nature with a certain geniality, which he managed to exploit for his own popularity, he was the most egocentric being imaginable. The assumption of political power was for him only a means to personal enrichment and personal good living. The success of others filled him with envy. His greed knew no bounds. His predilection for jewels, gold and finery, etcetera, was unimaginable. He knew no comradeship. Only as long as someone was useful to him did he profess friendship.*

*Göring's knowledge in all fields in which a government member should be competent was nil, especially in the economic field. Of all the economic matters which Hitler entrusted to him in the autumn of 1936 he had*

## CHAPTER TWELVE

*not the faintest notion, though he created an immense official apparatus and misused his powers as lord of all economy most outrageously. In his personal appearance he was so theatrical that one could only compare him with Nero. A lady who had tea with his second wife reported that he appeared at this tea in a sort of Roman toga and sandals studded with jewels, his fingers bedecked with innumerable jewelled rings and generally covered with ornaments, his face painted and his lips rouged.*

Schacht ran rings around Jackson in matters of economics. Then when Jackson commented on Schacht referring to Germany's former African colonies as 'our property', Schacht replied: 'Not I personally called them that. That is what the Treaty of Versailles calls them – "our property".'

Later he remarked: 'That is what happens when American prosecutors are sent over to Europe who don't even know anything about the Treaty of Versailles.'

Birkett said: 'Nothing occurred during the cross-examination other than a strengthening of Schacht's defence.'

The *New York Times* said that Schacht had slipped through Jackson's fingers and might well 'have won himself an acquittal'.

Schacht expected an instant dismissal of the charges against him. The next time he appeared in court he looked ten years younger and he told Gilbert that surely he would not be kept 'sitting here for another three months and listening to all that stuff that doesn't concern me'.

### *Walther Funk*
Funk was neither as intelligent nor as suave as his predecessor. Dodd had already read into testimony the decree he had signed after Kristallnacht, which imposed additional and

**The Money Men**

drastic economic disabilities upon the Jews, and subjected their property to confiscation and forced liquidation.

Dodd then referred to Funk's interrogation on 22 October 1945, in which he admitted that all decrees excluding Jews from economic life were his.

'The Party had always brought pressure to bear on me to make me agree to the confiscation of Jewish property, and I had refused repeatedly,' he had said. 'But, later on, when the anti-Jewish measures and the force against Jews came into effect, something legal had to be done to prevent the looting and confiscation of all Jewish property.'

He was then asked: 'You knew that the looting and all that was done at the instigation of the Party, did not you?'

The account of the interrogation then continued: 'Here defendant Funk wept, and answered: "Yes, most certainly. That is when I should have left, in 1938. Of that I am guilty; I am guilty; I admit that I am a guilty party here."'

## *Gold dentures*

In cross-examination Dodd asked: 'You were not ordinarily in the habit, in the Reichsbank, of accepting jewels, monocles, spectacles, watches, cigarette cases, pearls, diamonds, gold dentures, were you? You ordinarily accepted that sort of material for deposit in your bank?'

Funk replied that this would have been illegal. Those things were supposed to have been delivered to the Reich Office for Precious Metals. Funk said he knew nothing about this and never saw anything like that when he visited the vaults to view the gold deposits. Dodd then showed him a film taken in the vaults after the Allied invasion. Funk claimed that the things shown must have been valuables locked away in safety deposit boxes.

Dodd then asked: 'Did you ever hear of anybody depositing his gold dentures in a bank for safekeeping?'

## CHAPTER TWELVE

There was no response.

Dodd read an affidavit from Emil Puhl, vice-president of the Reichsbank.

*Funk told me that he had arranged with Reichsführer Himmler to have the Reichsbank receive in safe custody gold and jewels for the SS. Funk directed that I should work out the arrangements with Pohl, who, as head of the economic section of the SS, administered the economic side of the concentration camps. I asked Funk what the source was of the gold, jewels, banknotes, and other articles to be delivered by the SS. Funk replied that it was confiscated property from the Eastern Occupied Territories, and that I should ask no further questions. I protested against the Reichsbank handling this material. Funk stated that we were to go ahead with the arrangements for handling the material, and that we were to keep the matter absolutely secret ... The material deposited by the SS included jewellery, watches, eyeglass frames, dental gold, and other gold articles in great abundance, taken by the SS from Jews, concentration camp victims, and other persons. This was brought to our knowledge by SS personnel who attempted to convert this material into cash and who were helped in this by the Reichsbank personnel with Funk's approval and knowledge.*

## Chapter Thirteen
# War Horses

There was a certain sympathy for Dönitz. A sprinkling of British and American naval uniforms appeared in the courtroom. Nevertheless, according to the *Manchester Guardian*, he 'stared and turned pale when hearing evidence on refusing to rescue torpedoed sailors'.

Although an old-fashioned Prussian militarist, Dönitz was fanatical in his adherence to Hitler and the Nazi Party – according to the prosecution. In February 1944 he made a speech saying: 'From the very start the whole officer corps must be so indoctrinated that it feels itself co-responsible for the National Socialist State in its entirety. The officer is the exponent of the State; the idle chatter that the officer is non-political is sheer nonsense .... What would have become of our country today if the Führer had not united us under National Socialism? Split with parties, beset with the spreading poison of Jewry and vulnerable to it, and lacking as a defence our present and uncompromising ideology we would long since have succumbed to the burdens of this war and been subject to the merciless destruction of our adversaries.' This speech was not challenged when submitted as evidence by the prosecution.

Dönitz entered the witness box on the anniversary of VE Day and needed help to put on his headphones. The defence began by comparing British, American and German practice during the war, not on a *tu quoque* basis, but arguing that they were all legal.

## CHAPTER THIRTEEN

Dönitz said that he had not become Commander-in-Chief of the German Navy until 1943: consequently 'whether the leadership of the State was thereby politically waging an aggressive war or not, or whether they were protective measures, was not for me to decide; it was none of my business,' he maintained.

He also continued to claim that his meetings with Hitler were purely about naval matters and he knew nothing about

*Albert Speer and Admiral Karl Dönitz reviewing the U-boats that were aimed to starve Britain into surrender – and nearly succeeded.*

slave labour and the conditions in concentration camps. There was no evidence that he had enforced the commando order or ordered the killing of the survivors from the ships they had sunk. Dönitz left the witness box unbowed.

Soon after, a requested statement came from US Admiral Chester Nimitz, which stated that after the United States had entered the war, US submarines had attacked vessels without warning within designated theatres of operations and had not rescued enemy survivors where doing so would put their own vessels or missions at risk – in exactly the same way Dönitz had done.

## *Erich Raeder*

As Commander-in-Chief of the German Navy until 1943, Raeder faced the same charges as Dönitz. However, as he had commanded the navy in one form or another since 1928, the charge of waging an aggressive war was still outstanding.

He had not been present at key conferences and claimed to have built up the German Navy under the limits imposed by the Versailles Treaty, then the 1935 Anglo-German Naval Agreement, with only a few minor transgressions. His intentions were peaceful and he thought Hitler shared them.

He had not been party to the Anschluss and the invasion of Czechoslovakia. Over the Danzig corridor and Poland, he considered Hitler a 'master of bluff'. And Operation Barbarossa – the invasion of the Soviet Union – was a contingency plan. He considered it morally wrong to break the Molotov-Ribbentrop Pact, as well as stupid to fight on two fronts. And he had not wanted war with the United States.

'Since I was involved in a naval war with England with my small German Navy, I did not want ... to have America on my neck as well,' he said.

Maxwell Fyfe noted that 118 submarines were nearly completed by the outbreak of war, while Raeder and Dönitz said there were only 40 or so. Four warships had been deliberately heavier than their specification and Raeder had encouraged the German armaments industry to full production through exports, thus circumventing the restrictions of the Versailles Treaty, so it would be ready when war came. And he had issued an order to attack Soviet submarines six days before Operation Barbarossa began, on the excuse that he thought they were British. He also admitted passing on the Commando Order.

By this point, the trial had dragged on for six months and there was no end in sight. The Soviet newspaper *Izvestia* called it 'a slow-motion trial'.

### Von Schirach

As the leader of the Hitler Youth, Baldur von Schirach maintained that the uniforms they wore were 'the dress of comradeship', which helped break down class distinctions. Sports shooting with small-calibré arms was not prohibited by the Versailles Treaty. This was not militaristic. He quoted a British Board of Education pamphlet of 1938 saying: 'The worst that one can say of them is that they may be confidently recommended to the notice of any Boy Scout wishing to qualify for his marksmanship badge.'

He admitted that the SS and all German leadership corps recruited from the Hitler Youth. However, he said: 'The youth of Germany is guiltless. Our youth was anti-Semitically inclined, but it did not call for the extermination of Jewry. It neither realized nor imagined that Hitler had carried out this extermination by the daily murder of thousands of innocent people.'

At Auschwitz, Höss was merely the executioner, he maintained. The murder had been ordered by Hitler.

'The guilt is mine in that I educated the youth of Germany for a man who murdered by the millions,' he said. 'This is

## War Horses

*The prosecution contended that the Hitler Youth was not just the German equivalent of the Boy Scouts, but rather a training ground for new Nazis.*

my own – my own personal guilt. I was responsible for the youth of the country. I was placed in authority over the young people, and the guilt is mine alone. The younger generation ... grew up in an anti-Semitic state, ruled by anti-Semitic laws. Our youth was bound by these laws and saw nothing criminal in racial politics.'

Nevertheless, Schirach was loyal to Hitler to the end. He never betrayed him nor tried to overthrow him. He was a committed National Socialist and an anti-Semite.

### *Future soldiers*

Under cross-examination, Schirach admitted writing 'Forward, Forward', which, he said, was the flag song of the youth organization.

Dodd quoted the words: 'We are the future soldiers. Everything that opposes us will fall before our fists. Führer, we belong to you.'

Schirach said: 'I did not say: "We are the future soldiers" ... but "We are the soldiers of the future".'

He did not remember another song from the *Hitler Youth Song Book* whose second verse started: 'For many years the people were enslaved and misguided, traitors and Jews had the upper hand.' Another song was called 'People to Arms'. It contained the line: 'Germany awake! Death to Jewry! People to arms!' The first line was, tellingly: 'Can you see the dawn in the East?'

Schirach claimed not to know the song that contained the line 'Pope and Rabbi shall yield ... ' and maintained that a song that said 'We want to kill the priest, out with your spear ... ' dated back to the Thirty Years' War (1618–48).

Dodd handed him a telegram to Bormann in which Schirach had suggested an air raid on a 'cultural city' in Britain in retaliation for the assassination of SS General Reinhard Heydrich in Prague by a British-trained team. He asked: 'Were you thinking of some particular cultural city in Britain – like Cambridge, Oxford, Stratford, Canterbury?'

As well as being head of the Hitler Youth, Schirach had also been gauleiter of Vienna from 1940 onwards, when 60,000 Jews were deported to places in which he knew the mass murder of Jews was taking place. He received weekly reports from the SS on the activities of the Einsatzkommandos, though he claimed never to have read them. He visited Mauthausen and Dachau, which he said had a library and good medical facilities.

## *Sauckel*

In his defence, a document Sauckel had circulated to all German economic offices was read into the record. It said:

*In a number of the Eastern Territories indigenous male and female civilian labour working for the German war industry or the German Wehrmacht is undernourished. In the urgent interests of the German war industry in this territory this condition should be remedied. It is checking production and is dangerous. And endeavour must therefore be made by all means available to provide additional food for these workers and their families. This additional food must be given only in accordance with the output of work .... The foreign workers in the Reich and the population in the occupied territories who are being employed for the German war effort must be given the feeling that it is in their own interests to work loyally for Germany and that therein alone will they see and actually find their one real guarantee of life.*

Assistant French prosecutor Jacques Herzog asked: 'Did you ever consider that a worker could be taken to his work handcuffed?'

## CHAPTER THIRTEEN

Sauckel's answer was: 'Only if there were flagrant resistance to an executive authority.'

Herzog read an order issued by Sauckel that said: 'In more serious cases of absenteeism the district police authorities will submit the files concerning the cases to the competent Gestapo office (Cologne, Aachen or Bonn) for decision. The Gestapo will examine the matter and order the necessary measures – detention, sending to corrective labour camps or concentration camps.'

Sauckel insisted that he did not know of atrocities committed in concentration camps, though he admitted visiting Buchenwald. He claimed he had nothing to do with the deportation of Jews, though documents showed that he had organized the removal of Jews from factories and their replacement with 'other workers'. The Jews concerned were already prisoners of the SS.

He admitted that 5,124,000 people, including prisoners of war, had been brought into Germany from the occupied territories before 24 July 1942. In 1943, 1.5 to 2 million foreign workers were brought to Germany, in 1944 another 900,000. But at the end of the war, he said, there were 5 million. When Soviet prosecutor Alexandrov tried to establish how many had been worked to death, Sauckel insisted that many had simply gone home. A battle of numbers ensued. Eventually, Biddle had to intervene.

Witnesses called in Sauckel's defence said that the power lay with Speer. Sauckel simply supplied the workforce requested. The last witness called was Wilhelm Jaeger, a doctor at the Krupp works in Essen. He was of little help to the defence, speaking of an epidemic of typhus among the workers there, when there was no typhus in the German population. Tuberculosis was widespread, too.

In his affidavit, he said: 'The plan of supplies prescribed a little meat each week. Only Freibankfleisch could be used for this purpose, which was horse meat – meat infected with tuberculosis, or meat condemned by the veterinary.'

Freibankfleisch was unfit for human consumption.

He said that after an air raid 'the inmates for almost half a year were housed in dog kennels, latrines and old baking ovens'.

There were no tables, chairs or cupboards in the camp. This hardly aided the defence.

## Jodl

Keitel's deputy Alfred Jodl testified that he was not anti-Semitic and had only read parts of *Mein Kampf* after Hitler had come to power in 1933. Apart from the Golden Party Badge, he received nothing from Hitler or the Nazi Party during the five-and-a-half years of the war – though 'at headquarters we received a package of coffee from the Führer each Christmas'.

He read into the record his orders concerning partisans: 'All partisans captured in enemy uniform or civilian clothing or surrendering during combat are to be treated in principle as prisoners of war.'

When it came to the Commando Order, he agreed with Hitler that soldiers who behaved like bandits had put themselves outside the provisions of the Geneva Convention, though he set territorial limits on where it should be applied. However, he and other commanders-in-chief rejected lynching and the Commissar Order. Issued by Hitler on 6 June 1941, this commanded that captured Soviet political commissars be executed.

After two days' testimony, Jodl was cross-examined by British prosecutor G.D. 'Khaki' Roberts. He asked about the Anschluss: 'Austria, from that day, received all the benefits of National Socialism, is that right?'

## CHAPTER THIRTEEN

'That is a political question,' said Jodl. 'At any rate, it could perhaps have become the happiest country on earth.'

'I wasn't asking what it could have become, but what it received,' said Roberts. 'It received the SS, the Gestapo, the concentration camps, the suppression of opponents, and the persecution of Jews, didn't it?'

'Those are questions with which I did not concern myself,' said Jodl. 'Those questions you have to put to the competent authorities.'

He went on to say: 'The Polish campaign, from the military point of view, was extremely satisfactory to us.'

Otherwise Jodl continued to answer that the advances made through neutral countries were 'political questions' that did not concern him.

Throughout Jodl maintained the stance of a truthful and honourable – if unapologetic – man.

## Chapter Fourteen
# Pusillanimous Patriots

In Arthur Seyss-Inquart's defence, his counsel, Dr Gustav Steinbauer, read a quotation from a book by Roosevelt's under secretary of state Sumner Welles, *The Time for Decision*, detailing a conversation between Seyss-Inquart and the Italian foreign minister, Count Ciano: 'Before the occupation of Austria, Dr Schuschnigg [Chancellor of Austria] came to Rome. He admitted to me frankly that, if

*Left right: front row Wilhelm Frick, Julius Streicher, Walther Funk; back row – Franz von Papen, Arthur Seyss-Inquart, Albert Speer, Konstantin von Neurath.*

## CHAPTER FOURTEEN

Germany occupied Austria, the majority of Austrians would support the occupation and, if Italy sent troops into Austria to prevent the occupation, the Austrians as one man would join with the Germans to fight Italy.'

While Chancellor Kurt Schuschnigg made his farewell speech on 11 March 1938, having been forced from office, 40 SS men armed with pistols occupied his office. Seyss-Inquart then took over.

The defendant addressed his time as Reich commissioner of the Netherlands, where he closed down chess clubs on the grounds that they were political. He admitted sending Jews from the Netherlands to Auschwitz, but had insisted that they be allowed to write home.

'For about three quarters of a year or a year correspondence was maintained; not only short post cards but long letters were permitted,' he said. 'I do not know how the camp administration did this; but the letters were identified as authentic by the addressee. When the number of letters dropped off later – it never stopped completely – the Security Police told me that the Jews in Auschwitz now had fewer acquaintances in the Netherlands, meaning other Jews, because most of them were already in Auschwitz.'

He said he realized that they would suffer because of the shortage of food and, or course, families would be torn apart.

The cross-examination was carried out by French prosecutor Delphin Debenest, who concentrated on Seyss-Inquart's time in the Netherlands where, among other things, he seized the treasury and appointed a Dutch Nazi president of the Bank of Holland. He also took charge of the curriculum of Dutch schools, which he thought was anti-German. Universities were also closed down after students went on strike in Leiden over the sacking of Jewish professors. Attempts to make the University of Leiden a National Socialist university failed when all the professors

## Pusillanimous Patriots

resigned in protest at National Socialists being appointed to their faculties. Suspect professors were sent to St Michelsgestel.

'That is this concentration camp where the inmates played golf,' said Seyss-Inquart.

Students were then liable for forced labour. He admitted that he enrolled 250,000 Dutch people to work in Germany, though contested a document that said he had suggested Jews who wanted to stay in Holland should be sterilized.

He denied the shooting of hostages – they were 'rather executions carried out by the police on the basis of a Führer decree'. The evidence against Seyss-Inquart then ran into difficulties, because much of it was in Dutch. Four languages was all the tribunal could cope with. Despite Seyss-Inquart's denials, it was plain that there had been numerous examples of the shooting of hostages while he had been in command in the Netherlands. In one case he was insistent that he had only had five men shot, rather than the 25 called for.

'I saved fathers of several children from being shot,' he said.

On another occasion he approved the shooting of 230 Dutchmen after an assassination attempt on a German official. But, he insisted, these men had already been condemned to death for sabotage. When instances of people being arrested and summarily shot were brought up, Seyss-Inquart denied all responsibility.

'These shootings,' he said, 'cannot be traced to my directives and my summary justice courts, but rather to a direct decree of the Führer' – although, of course, Seyss-Inquart approved.

Under cross-examination it was shown that Seyss-Inquart was also responsible for commandeering foodstuffs for the Reich, resulting in the starvation of the Dutch, and confiscating the property of Freemasons. Nine million guilders were handed over to the Nazi Party. Another 400 million guilders were raised by the 'Aryanization' of Jewish property. That money went to the Administrative Office for Property and Pensions, but was not used for the benefit of the Reich, he insisted, but rather to build a 'Jewish assembly camp'.

## *Von Papen*

In his defence, von Papen portrayed himself as a patriot who had been forced to recognize that the Nazis were a major political force and, at a time when law and order were rapidly disintegrating, that it was his duty to help Hitler come to power in 1933. However, he had criticized Nazi methods in a speech he made at Marburg University the following year.

Two weeks later, on the 'Night of the Long Knives', Göring told him 'in the interests of my own safety, as he said, to return to my apartment and stay there. I protested quite vehemently against this demand, but Herr Göring insisted. On my way back to my apartment, I went first to my office in the Vice Chancellery. On arriving there, I found my office occupied by the SS, and I was permitted only to enter my own room and get my files. I went on home to my apartment, where I found a large number of SS. The telephone was disconnected; the radio was disconnected; and I was completely cut off from the outside world for three whole days.'

His press adviser was shot in his office. Another colleague also died and three were sent to a concentration camp. He resigned as vice-chancellor. Sent as ambassador to Austria on the very day his friend, the Austrian chancellor Engelbert Dollfuss, had been assassinated by the Nazis, von Papen said he 'demanded an assurance in writing from Hitler that the German-Austrian policy of the future – what is generally termed the Anschluss policy – would move on a purely evolutionary level, that is to say, that no recourse would be had to forcible measures and aggression'. When the Anschluss went ahead anyway, von Papen was made ambassador to Turkey. Consequently, he was not charged with war crimes or crimes against humanity, only conspiracy and commissioning a war of aggression.

### 'Greatest crook'

Maxwell Fyfe opened his cross-examination by quoting von Papen's interrogation in September where he had said that Hitler was the greatest crook he had ever seen in his life, but had come to that conclusion 'only after I have known the facts after which he started to go to war'. Maxwell Fyfe then sought to show that von Papen had had the opportunity to reach that conclusion much earlier. Indeed, Hitler's intentions had been made clear to him in 1932, when as chancellor he had sought to make Hitler vice-chancellor, but he had refused.

Maxwell Fyfe then read a letter that von Papen had written to Hitler directly after the 'Night of the Long Knives', when two of his close colleagues had been murdered, addressing him as 'Most honoured Reich Chancellor' and signing off 'With unchanged admiration and loyalty ....'

'Why did you write stuff like that to the head of a gang of murderers who had murdered your collaborators?' asked Maxwell Fyfe. Pressing the matter, he said: 'Herr von Papen, if you, as an ex-Chancellor of the Reich and, as you said yourself, one of the leading Catholic laymen of Germany, an ex-officer of the Imperial Army, had said at that time "I am not going to be associated with murder, cold-blooded murder as an instrument of policy," you might at some risk to yourself have brought down the whole of this rotten regime, might you not?'

'That is possible, but had I said it publicly, then quite probably I would have disappeared somewhere just as my associates did,' von Papen replied. 'Apart from that, the

## CHAPTER FOURTEEN

world knew from my resignation that I did not identify myself with this affair.'

When von Papen denied knowledge of other murders and brutality in prisons and concentration camps, Maxwell Fyfe produced evidence that he was aware of it.

'You had seen your own friends, your own servants, murdered around you. You had the detailed knowledge of it, and the only reason that could have led you on and made you take one job after another from the Nazis was that you sympathized with their work. That is what I am putting against you, Herr von Papen,' said Maxwell Fyfe.

'That, Sir David, is perhaps your opinion,' replied von Papen. 'My opinion is that I am responsible only to my conscience and to the German people for my decision to work for my fatherland; and I shall accept their verdict.'

### Speer

As Reichminister for armaments and munitions, Speer admitted that he knew most members of the workforce he employed were forced labour. It was Sauckel's job to provide him with workers. How he recruited them was 'no concern of mine'. Nor were the working conditions his responsibility.

Speer realized that the war was lost when Allied bombing began attacking fuel plants. He told Hitler his opinion, writing 12 memoranda about it between June and December 1944.

'The sacrifices which were made on both sides after January 1945 were senseless,' he said. 'The dead of this period will be the accusers of the man responsible for the continuation of that fight, Adolf Hitler. The same is true of the ruined cities, which in this last phase had to lose tremendous cultural values and where innumerable dwellings suffered destruction.'

He also blamed Hitler for 'the ruthless destruction of

## Pusillanimous Patriots

bridges, traffic installations, trucks, locomotives and ships. The German people remained loyal to Adolf Hitler until the end. He betrayed them with intent. He tried to throw them definitely into the abyss.'

Speer's counsel Dr Hans Flachsner then asked him about his plot to assassinate Hitler, Bormann and Goebbels in February 1945. Speer replied, perhaps disingenuously: 'I am most unwilling to describe the details because there is always something repellent about such matters. I do it only because it is the tribunal's wish.'

He explained: 'Since 20 July it was no longer possible even for Hitler's closest associates to enter this shelter without their pockets and briefcases being examined by the SS for explosives.'

But as an architect he knew Hitler's bunker well. It had an air-conditioning system. He obtained some poison gas (this was supported by an affidavit from the underling who had supplied it). However, 'when the time came, I inspected the ventilator shaft in the garden of the Chancellery along with Hanschel; and there I discovered that on Hitler's personal order this ventilator had recently been surrounded by a chimney 4 meters high. That can still be ascertained today. Due to this it was no longer possible to carry out my plan.'

Göring told the other defendants that if Speer were not hanged by this court, then another would inflict the death penalty for treason.

### *Slackers*

Jackson led the cross-examination. He got Speer to admit to having used the threat of being sent to a concentration camp to encourage 'slackers'. Speer also admitted that 100,000 Jews from Hungary had been used in underground aircraft factories.

## CHAPTER FOURTEEN

As for foreign workers: 'I had no objection to their being brought to Germany against their will. On the contrary, during the first period, until the autumn of 1942, I certainly also took some pains to see that as many workers as possible should be brought to Germany in this manner.'

He was dismissive about the use of prisoners of war in armaments factories, though it was a clear violation of the Geneva Convention. Documentary evidence was introduced that showed Speer was also prepared to ignore the Hague conventions.

When shown steel whips that had been issued to guards at labour camps, he explained that they were merely replacements for rubber trncheons, because there was a shortage of rubber.

Though Speer repeatedly dodged responsibility for specific crimes in the system of forced labour he oversaw,

*The use of forced labour was clearly a crime against humanity. Workers were seized from their home countries, taken to Germany and often brutally maltreated.*

he was prepared to take overall responsibility as a member of the government. But these were weasel words.

'This common responsibility, however, can only be applied to fundamental matters,' he said. 'It cannot be applied to details connected with other ministries or other responsible departments, for otherwise the entire discipline in the life of the State would be quite confused, and no one would ever know who is individually responsible in a particular sphere. This individual responsibility in one's own sphere must, at all events, be kept clear and distinct.'

## *Von Neurath*

At the age of 74, von Neurath was the oldest of the defendants and, like von Papen, he presented himself as an aristocrat who had simply done his duty to the state. He had joined von Papen's cabinet as foreign minister in 1932 and remained in government under Hitler until he was sacked in 1938 to make way for Ribbentrop, though he claimed to have resigned when he learned of Hitler's belligerent intentions – which he believed would lead to world war. However, he kept the title 'Reichminister' and, during the Anschluss, he stood in for Ribbentrop because he was away.

Von Neurath was not a member of the Nazi Party or an anti-Semite.

'My Christian and humanitarian convictions prevented that,' he said. 'A repression of the undue Jewish influence in all spheres of public and cultural life, as it had developed after the First World War in Germany, however, I regarded as desirable.'

He admitted knowing about the invasion of Czechoslovakia beforehand and that Hitler made him Reichsprotektor of Bohemia and Moravia, though on false terms.

'He assured me that he would support me in every way and at all times in my work of settling the national conflicts

## CHAPTER FOURTEEN

justly and winning over the Czechs by a conciliatory and moderate policy,' said von Neurath. 'In particular, he would protect my administration from all attacks by political radicals, above all by the SS and police and Sudeten Germans; I had pointed out this danger particularly.'

Von Neurath said that he had the impression that Hitler was 'serious and honest' in his assurances for the humane treatment of the Czechs. He also claimed to know nothing of Hitler's planned 'forcible Germanization' of the Czechs. He considered the war 'the greatest piece of stupidity', believing from the outset that Britain would keep her promise to Poland and that once Britain and France had declared war, the United States, with its huge productive capacity, would stand behind them. He had told Hitler his opinion that the war was 'insanity', but he did not resign because 'through my remaining in office I wanted ... to prevent a harsher treatment of the Czech population by the policy of conciliation and compromise which I followed'.

Maxwell Fyfe asked why when just six weeks after Hitler came to power the 'Brown Terror' (in which tens of thousands of Jews, Communists and Social Democrats were arrested and maltreated) began, von Neurath did not bring the matter up in Cabinet? Von Neurath replied that he thought the stories were propaganda; the newspapers often got things wrong. He began to stutter. Maxwell Fyfe asked if von Neurath had tried to check out the veracity of the newspaper stories.

'Did you ask Himmler, or did you ask the defendant Göring?'

'Most certainly not,' he replied.

Asked whether he protested in Cabinet about the suppression of opposition parties and the trades unions, he replied that he was foreign minister, not the minister of the interior. It was none of his business. However, he claimed that he raised his objections personally with Hitler again and again.

'Did you ever hear that every cabinet minister must leave the cabinet if he does not agree with one particular thing?' said von Neurath.

'Every cabinet minister for whom I have any respect left a cabinet if it did something of which he morally disapproved,' said Maxwell Fyfe.

As foreign minister then, Maxwell Fyfe said, von Neurath had overseen Germany's withdrawal from the League of Nations and the World Disarmament Conference in Geneva.

'May I take it, that up to the end of 1933, despite these matters which I have put to you, that you were perfectly satisfied with the respectability and peace-loving intentions of the government; is that right?'

'Yes,' said von Neurath.

He claimed to be repulsed by the bloodletting on the 'Night of the Long Knives', but when asked by Maxwell Fyfe why he stayed on in a government that used murder as an instrument of policy, he replied: 'Such mishaps cannot be avoided, most unfortunately.'

Foreign office staff in the embassy in Vienna connived in the assassination of Chancellor Dollfuss. The German government had exported its policy of murder, but still von Neurath did not resign.

'If I were responsible for every single murderer, for every single German murderer who was active abroad, then I would have had a lot of work to do, would I not?' von Neurath protested.

## The Germanization of Czechoslovakia

Maxwell Fyfe elicited further protests when he sought to show that, as foreign minister, von Neurath must have known of Hitler's intentions towards the Rhineland, Austria and Czechoslovakia. The prosecutor also established that,

## CHAPTER FOURTEEN

as Reichsprotektor in Czechoslovakia, he persecuted the Church there.

Evidence was presented that both von Neurath and Rosenberg had taken possession of houses from the 'non-Aryan' residents by the simple expedient of turning up with a uniformed SA or SS man. Then Maxwell Fyfe read a memorandum from von Neurath to the Reich Chancellery, explaining his plans for Czechoslovakia.

'The most radical and theoretically complete solution to the problem would be to evacuate all Czechs completely from this country and replace them by Germans,' it said.

However, this would not be possible because there were not sufficient Germans to fill it. So von Neurath proposed 'keeping those Czechs who are suitable for Germanization by individual selective breeding, while on the other hand ... expelling those who are not useful from a racial standpoint or are enemies of the Reich'. These, particularly, included the intelligentsia who, he complained, 'more or less openly ... sabotage or at any rate postpone necessary measures'.

'If we use such a procedure, Germanization can be carried out successfully,' the memorandum continued.

Getting rid of the teachers, writers and singers of Czechoslovakia, the people who handed down the history and traditions of the Czech people to future generations, amounted to genocide. Von Neurath said that he had not written the memorandum, but had simply appended his name to it.

Maxwell Fyfe went on to show that von Neurath agreed with changes in education dedicated to the 'extermination of the Czech historical myth' – right back to the time of St Wenceslaus; closing Czech universities, and ultimately schools; a campaign against the Czech language; 'racial examination' before marriage; compulsory labour service; and 'after a victorious war' the assimilation of Czechoslovakia into the Greater German Reich. Although the documentary evidence showed von Neurath to have agreed with these proposals, he claimed that in private he had told Hitler he didn't. However, Hitler certainly subscribed to them.

## *Fritzsche*

The last defendant in the dock was Hans Fritzsche. He was also the lowest-ranking of the defendants. In 1933 he joined the Nazi Party and became head of the news service in the press section of the ministry of propaganda, briefing editors on what they should put in their newspapers. In 1937, he started making propaganda broadcasts, becoming head of the radio division of the ministry in 1942.

The case against him was weak. He had never met Hitler nor most of his fellow defendants before they ended up in the dock together. The prosecution contended that he had helped win the German people over to the aggressive aims of the Nazis. Broadcasting as the Wehrmacht rolled into the Soviet Union, he had said: 'In the struggle in the East ... culture, civilization and human decency make a stand against the diabolical principle of the subhuman world.'

The problem for the prosecution was to show that his words provoked any particular criminal action. Creating propaganda is not in itself an offence. Worse, the evidence was thin. Fritzsche had improvised his broadcasts from sketchy notes that had not been preserved. The broadcasts themselves had not been recorded. The BBC had monitored them, but had only kept extracts transcribed in English.

He had come to the attention of the Soviets and was used to identify the body of Goebbels, his boss. In the notorious Lubyanka prison in Moscow, he had been forced to sign a confession, which was so clearly not his own words that the other prosecutors were reluctant to use it and when his counsel offered an affidavit in its place they readily agreed.

Fritzsche was popular among the other defendants. As

a professional broadcaster, he coached them in giving their testimony.

His own performance on the witness stand was rambling and lacklustre, however. He admitted urging 'the necessity and obligation to fight' and to being anti-Semitic. He knew of the existence of concentration camps from official communiqués. However, he said: 'If the German people had learned of these mass murders, they would certainly no longer have supported Hitler. They would probably have sacrificed five million for a victory, but never would the German people have wished to bring about victory by the murder of five million people. I should like to state further that this murder decree of Hitler's seems to me the end of every race theory, every race philosophy, every kind of race propaganda, for after this catastrophe, any further advocacy of race theory would be equivalent to approval in theory of further murder. An ideology in the name of which five million people were murdered is one which cannot continue to exist.'

## Lied to the people

He criticized Goebbels for repeatedly assuring him that Hitler was trying to end the war and said: 'I am convinced that Hitler and at least some of his colleagues had deliberately lied to the people ... right from the beginning of their political career.'

Fritzsche admitted that, before the war, he had believed in dictatorship for a 'temporary emergency period'. He had now changed his mind.

'After the totalitarian form of government has brought about the catastrophe of the murder of five millions, I consider this form of government wrong even in times of emergency,' he said. 'I believe any kind of democratic control, even a restricted democratic control, would have made such a catastrophe impossible.'

He also denied using the term 'master race' and said that he 'expressly prohibited this term being used by the German press and the German radio when I was in charge of one or the other'. Nor had he called the Polish or Russian people 'subhuman'. When Rudenko put this accusation to him, he pointed out that no witnesses had been called to attest to his endorsement of racial theory.

'You remember, I hope, the testimony of the witness Höss regarding the extermination of millions of persons,' said the Soviet prosecutor.

'I did not forget this testimony,' said Fritzsche, 'and not for a minute did it escape my memory.'

### Bormann

'The Bormann case is characterized by the fact that not only the defendant cannot be found but almost all the witnesses cannot be found either,' said Bormann's defence counsel Dr Friedrich Bergold.

He had applied for several witnesses, most of whom were to testify that Bormann was dead. One of them had been released from a camp to appear and seized the opportunity to abscond. What little evidence Bergold had was presented in the form of documents, which took less than a day.

### Katyn Forest

At the Soviets' insistence, the murders in the Katyn Forest had been included on the indictment, much to the embarrassment of the other prosecutors. Nevertheless, two days were given over to it.

The Soviet prosecutors maintained that the killings had been carried out by Engineer Battalion 537 under the command of Colonel Friedrich Ahrens. He was called to the stand by Dr Stahmer.

Ahrens admitted that his unit – Signal Regiment 537 – had

## CHAPTER FOURTEEN

been in the vicinity of the Katyn Forest, arriving there in the autumn of 1941. But he had only two or three officers, and some 18–20 non-commissioned officers and men under him. They were fully occupied manning telephones and teleprinters.

He said that he had received no orders to shoot Poles, nor had any been shot on his instructions. However, his soldiers pointed out a mound with a birch cross on it. They told him that shootings had taken place there. Early in 1943, a wolf had been scratching at the earth there and had dug up what turned out to be human bones.

Exhumations were undertaken by a Professor Butz, who determined that the shootings had taken place in the spring of 1940. A Russian couple who lived nearby said that more than 200 uniformed Poles had been taken there in trucks in the spring of 1940 and they had heard lots of screams and shots.

According to the Soviet prosecutors, the killings had taken place in the autumn of 1941 when the Germans had invaded, not in the spring of 1940 when the Soviet Union held that area.

Lieutenant Reinhard von Eichborn, also with Signal Regiment 537, likewise testified that there was no Engineer Battalion 537 and there were no secret orders to a special Einsatzgruppe in the area to murder Polish prisoners of war as a Soviet report alleged.

Stahmer then called Lieutenant General Eugen Oberhauser – Signal Regiment 537 was part of his command. He, again, said that there were no orders to shoot prisoners of war. He knew nothing of Polish prisoners of war being in German hands when he was in that area in September 1941 and, if 11,000 Polish PoWs had been murdered there, they would not have been buried so close to his headquarters.

As a signal regiment, Regiment 537 would have been spread out and not concentrated in one place as would be

## Pusillanimous Patriots

*The Soviets insisted that the massacre of Polish officers in the Katyn Forest be included on the indictment although it had been done by the Soviets themselves.*

necessary to carry out such a massacre. They did not have the automatic weapons required, nor were the weapons they did have of the same calibre as those used to kill the Poles. And he knew nothing of an Einsatzgruppe in that area at that time.

The examination of the massacre in the Katyn Forest went nowhere, but its investigation was not the job of the tribunal. It had only been included at the insistence of the Soviet delegation – who sought to blame the Nazis. No mention was made of it in the judgment.

In 1992, after the collapse of the Soviet Union, the Russian government released documents proving that the Soviet politburo and their secret police, the NKVD, were responsible for the massacre and its cover-up.

## Chapter Fifteen
# Closing Speeches

The court had now been sitting for more than 170 days and the bench was anxious to bring proceedings to a speedy conclusion. To avoid needless repetition, defence counsels were limited to half a day for their closing arguments. These were to be handed over in advance, so they could be cut if necessary. Steinbauer was asked to remove a page and a half on the influence of Beethoven and Brahms on the cultural life of Vienna. In the courtroom Lawrence said: 'I think it is possible for the tribunal to become acquainted with the history of Austria without having it read to them as a part of your argument.'

Sections entitled 'The Development of the History of the Intellectual Pursuit' and 'Renaissance, Subjectivism, the French Revolution and National Socialism' were cut from Kaufmann's speech.

Lawrence chastised him further in court, saying: 'Dr Kaufmann, the tribunal proposes, as far as it can, to decide the cases which it has got to decide in accordance with law and not with the sort of very general, very vague and misty philosophical doctrine with which you appear to be dealing in the first twelve pages of your speech, and, therefore ... they would very much prefer that you begin on page thirteen.'

Nevertheless, Kaufmann was able to get away with a passage that began: 'The deepest and at the same time most fatal reason for the Hitler phenomenon lies in the metaphysical domain ....'

Rebecca West declared: 'The courtroom was a citadel of boredom.' She also described it as 'water-torture, boredom falling drop by drop on the same spot of the soul'; 'the symbol of Nuremberg was a yawn' and that 'this was boredom on a huge historic scale.'

Professor Hermann Jahrreiss, assistant counsel for Jodl, was also allowed to address general legal matters brought up by the defence. First he argued that the tribunal could hardly be impartial, because the judges represented the victors while the defendants were the vanquished. However, the Charter prohibited any challenge to the validity of the tribunal.

Secondly, the waging of aggressive war had not previously been a crime. The Kellogg-Briand Pact had condemned but not outlawed it. This issue had been addressed in the prosecution's opening speeches. Further laws were supposed to be applied in general, not devised for a single special case, nor was there a precedent in international law for individuals being held responsible for acts committed by a state.

Then there was the Führerprinzip – the leadership system in the Third Reich, whereby all orders emanated from Adolf Hitler. Reading the advanced copy of Jahrreiss's speech, Maxwell Fyfe said that the Führerprinzip was merely the disguised pleading of obeying superiors orders, ruled out by the Charter.

## *The resurrection of Jackson*

Jackson was still smarting from the mauling that Göring had given him. But in his closing statement for the prosecution, he returned to the rhetorical heights he had scaled at the outset.

'In eight months – a short time as state trials go – we have introduced evidence which embraces as vast and varied a panorama of events as has ever been compressed within the framework of a litigation,' he said. 'It is impossible in

## CHAPTER FIFTEEN

summation to do more than outline with bold strokes the vitals of this trial's mad and melancholy record, which will live as the historical text of the twentieth century's shame and depravity.'

He dismissed any challenge to the legitimacy of the proceedings.

'The defendants denounce the law under which their accounting is asked. Their dislike for the law which condemns them is not original. It has been remarked before that "No thief e'er felt the halter draw with good opinion of the law." ...

'Of one thing we may be sure. The future will never have to ask, with misgiving, what could the Nazis have said in their favour. History will know that whatever could be said, they were allowed to say. They have been given the kind of a trial which they, in the days of their pomp and power, never gave to any man.'

Summarizing the case, he showed that the defendants were joined in a conspiracy by the way they seized power and subjugated Germany, turning it into a police state. Jackson seized the opportunity to take a swing at Göring, who had announced publicly in 1933: 'Whoever in the future raises a hand against a representative of the National Socialist movement or of the State must know that he will lose his life in a very short while.'

Their enemies were legion. 'Therefore, the concentration camps have been created, where we have first confined thousands of Communists and social democrat functionaries,' Göring had said the following year.

They began their preparations to wage wars of aggression in contravention of the Versailles Treaty as soon as they seized power. And four days after Japan had attacked without warning at Pearl Harbor, Germany declared war on the United States without provocation.

## Closing Speeches

The defendants had deliberately breached both the Hague and Geneva conventions to which Germany was party, violating the rules of war. They had plundered the countries they had occupied and enslaved their people. And they had persecuted and murdered Jews and Christians: he detailed some of the crimes, then quoted the defendans condemning themselves out of their own mouths.

*The testimony of the survivors of the concentration camps was irrefutable. None of the defendants was able to counter it.*

'These, then, were the five great substantive crimes of the Nazi regime,' Jackson said. 'Their commission, which cannot be denied, stands admitted.'

## CHAPTER FIFTEEN

### *Criminals*

He then turned his attention to the individual defendants in the dock.

'Göring was half militarist and half gangster,' he said. 'He stuck his pudgy finger in every pie ....

'The zealot Hess, before succumbing to wanderlust, was the engineer tending the Party machinery, passing orders and propaganda down to the Leadership Corps, supervising every aspect of Party activities, and maintaining the organization as a loyal and ready instrument of power ....

'The duplicitous Ribbentrop, the salesman of deception ... was detailed to pour wine on the troubled waters of suspicion by preaching the gospel of limited and peaceful intentions.

'Keitel, the weak and willing tool, delivered the Armed Forces, the instrument of aggression, over to the Party and directed them in executing its felonious designs.

'Kaltenbrunner, the grand inquisitor, took up the bloody mantle of Heydrich to stifle opposition and terrorize compliance, and buttressed the power of National Socialism on a foundation of guiltless corpses.

'It was Rosenberg, the intellectual high priest of the "master race", who provided the doctrine of hatred which gave the impetus for the annihilation of Jewry, and who put his infidel theories into practice against the Eastern Occupied Territories. His woolly philosophy also added boredom to the long list of Nazi atrocities.

'The fanatical Frank, who solidified Nazi control by establishing the new order of authority without law, so that the will of the Party was the only test of legality, proceeded to export his lawlessness to Poland, which he governed with the lash of Caesar and whose population he reduced to sorrowing remnants.

'Frick, the ruthless organizer, helped the Party to seize

power, supervised the police agencies to ensure that it stayed in power, and chained the economy of Bohemia and Moravia to the German war machine.

'Streicher, the venomous Bulgarian, manufactured and distributed obscene racial libels which incited the populace to accept and assist the progressively savage operations of "race purification".

'As minister of economics Funk accelerated the pace of rearmament, and as Reichsbank president banked for the SS the gold teeth-fillings of concentration camp victims – probably the most ghoulish collateral in banking history.

'It was Schacht, the facade of starched respectability, who in the early days provided the window dressing, the bait for the hesitant, and whose wizardry later made it possible for Hitler to finance the colossal rearmament program, and to do it secretly.

'Dönitz, Hitler's legatee of defeat, promoted the success of the Nazi aggressions by instructing his pack of submarine killers to conduct warfare at sea with the illegal ferocity of the jungle.

'Raeder, the political admiral, stealthily built up the German Navy in defiance of the Versailles Treaty, and then put it to use in a series of aggressions which he had taken a leading part in planning.

'Sauckel, the greatest and cruellest slaver since the pharaohs of Egypt, produced desperately needed manpower by driving foreign peoples into the land of bondage on a scale unknown even in the ancient days of tyranny in the kingdom of the Nile.

'Jodl, betrayer of the traditions of his profession, led the Wehrmacht in violating its own code of military honour in order to carry out the barbarous aims of Nazi policy.

'Von Papen, pious agent of an infidel regime, held the stirrup while Hitler vaulted into the saddle, lubricated the

## CHAPTER FIFTEEN

Austrian annexation and devoted his diplomatic cunning to the service of Nazi objectives abroad.

'Von Schirach, poisoner of a generation, initiated the German youth in Nazi doctrine, trained them in legions for service in the SS and Wehrmacht and delivered them up to the Party as fanatic, unquestioning executors of its will.

'Seyss-Inquart, spearhead of the Austrian fifth column, took over the government of his own country only to make a present of it to Hitler, and then, moving north, brought terror and oppression to the Netherlands and pillaged its economy for the benefit of the German juggernaut.

'Von Neurath, the old-school diplomat, who cast the pearls of his experience before Nazis, guided Nazi diplomacy in the early years, soothed the fears of prospective victims, and, as Reich Protector of Bohemia and Moravia, strengthened the German position for the coming attack on Poland.

'Speer, as minister of armaments and production, joined in planning and executing the programme to dragoon prisoners of war and foreign workers into German war industries, which waxed in output while the labourers waned in starvation.

'Fritzsche, radio propaganda chief, by manipulation of the truth goaded German public opinion into frenzied support of the regime and anesthetized the independent judgement of the population so that they did without question their masters' bidding.

'And Bormann, who has not accepted our invitation to this reunion, sat at the throttle of the vast and powerful engine of the Party, guiding it in the ruthless execution of Nazi policies, from the scourging of the Christian Church to the lynching of captive Allied airmen.'

### The Führer principle

Jackson also dismissed the defence of the Führerprinzip effortlessly.

'I admit that Hitler was the chief villain,' he said. 'But for the defendants to put all blame on him is neither manly nor true. We know that even the head of the state has the same limits to his senses and to the hours of his days as do lesser men. He must rely on others to be his eyes and ears as to most that goes on in a great empire. Other legs must run his errands; other hands must execute his plans. On whom did Hitler rely for such things more than upon these men in the dock? Who led him to believe he had an invincible air armada if not Göring? Who kept disagreeable facts from him? Did not Göring forbid Field Marshal Milch to warn Hitler that in his opinion Germany was not equal to the war upon Russia? ... Who led Hitler, utterly untravelled himself, to believe in the indecision and timidity of

*It was clear that Hitler's generals knew that he intended to start an aggressive war. None of them stood in his way or advised against it.*

democratic peoples if not Ribbentrop, von Neurath and von Papen? Who fed his illusion of German invincibility i not Keitel, Jodl, Raeder and Dönitz? Who kept his hatred of the Jews inflamed more than Streicher and Rosenberg? Who would Hitler say deceived him about conditions in concentration camps if not Kaltenbrunner, even as he would deceive us?'

## False statements and double talk

Jackson went on to demolish whatever other arguments they had put up on their defence.

'Besides outright false statements and double talk, there are also other circumventions of truth in the nature of fantastic explanations and absurd professions,' said Jackson. 'Streicher has solemnly maintained that his only thought with respect to the Jews was to resettle them on the island of Madagascar. His reason for destroying synagogues, he blandly said, was only because they were architecturally offensive. Rosenberg was stated by his counsel to have always had in mind a "chivalrous solution" to the Jewish problem. When it was necessary to remove Schuschnigg after the Anschluss, Ribbentrop would have had us believe that the Austrian Chancellor was resting at a "villa". It was left to cross-examination to reveal that the "villa" was Buchenwald concentration camp. The record is full of other examples of dissimulations and evasions. Even Schacht showed that he, too, had adopted the Nazi attitude that truth is any story which succeeds. Confronted on cross-examination with a long record of broken vows and false words, he declared in justification – and I quote from the record: "I think you can score many more successes when you want to lead someone if you don't tell them the truth than if you tell them the truth."

'This was the philosophy of the National Socialists. When for years they have deceived the world, and masked falsehood with plausibilities, can anyone be surprised that they continue their habits of a lifetime in this dock? Credibility is one of the main issues of this trial. Only those who have failed to learn the bitter lessons of the last decade can doubt that men who have always played on the unsuspecting credulity of generous opponents would not hesitate to do the same, now.'

Jackson concluded with a Shakespearean flourish, saying: 'It is against such a background that these defendants now ask this tribunal to say that they are not guilty of planning, executing or conspiring to commit this long list of crimes and wrongs. They stand before the record of this trial as bloodstained Gloucester stood by the body of his slain king. He begged of the widow, as they beg of you: "Say I slew them not." And the Queen replied, "Then say they were not slain. But dead they are ... " If you were to say of these men that they are not guilty, it would be as true to say that there has been no war, there are no slain, there has been no crime.'

## Sir Hartley Shawcross

Returning from his duties as attorney general in Britain, Sir Hartley Shawcross gave the closing address for the British delegation.

While Shawcross admitted that they were there to determine the legal guilt of the defendants, there were wider considerations.

'That these defendants participated in and are morally guilty of crimes so frightful that the imagination staggers and reels back at their very contemplation is not in doubt,' he said. 'Let the words of the defendant Frank, which were repeated to you this morning, be well remembered:

## CHAPTER FIFTEEN

"Thousands of years will pass and this guilt of Germany will not be erased." Total and totalitarian war, waged in defiance of solemn undertakings and in breach of treaties; great cities, from Coventry to Stalingrad, reduced to rubble, the countryside laid waste and now the inevitable aftermath of war so fought – hunger and disease stalking through the world; millions of people homeless, maimed, bereaved.

'And in their graves, crying out, not for vengeance but that this shall not happen again: 10 million who might be living in peace and happiness at this hour, soldiers, sailors, airmen and civilians killed in battles that ought never to have been.

'Nor was that the only or the greatest crime. In all our countries when perhaps in the heat of passion or for other motives which impair restraint some individual is killed, the murder becomes a sensation, our compassion is aroused, nor do we rest until the criminal is punished and the rule of law is vindicated. Shall we do less when not one but on the lowest computation twelve million men, women and children, are done to death? Not in battle, not in passion, but in the cold, calculated, deliberate attempt to destroy nations and races, to disintegrate the traditions, the institutions and the very existence of free and ancient states. Twelve million murders. Two-thirds of the Jews in Europe exterminated, more than six million of them on the killers' own figures. Murder conducted like some mass production industry in the gas chambers and the ovens of Auschwitz, Dachau, Treblinka, Buchenwald, Mauthausen, Majdanek and Oranienburg.

'And is the world to overlook the revival of slavery in Europe, slavery on a scale which involved seven million men, women and children taken from their homes, treated as beasts, starved, beaten and murdered?'

## Acts of aggression

He went on to list the acts of aggression committed by Nazi Germany up to and including the invasion of the Soviet Union in 1941.

'In no single case did a declaration of war precede military action,' said Shawcross. 'How many thousands of innocent, inoffensive men, women and children, sleeping in their beds in the happy belief that their country was and would remain at peace, were suddenly blown into eternity by death dropped on them without warning from the skies? In what respect does the guilt of any one of these men differ from the common murderer creeping stealthily to do his victims to death in order that he may rob them of their belongings?

'In every single case, as the documents make clear, this was the common plan.'

Then quoting the documents, he said: 'The attack must be "*blitzartig schnell*" – without warning, with the speed of lightning – Austria, Czechoslovakia, Poland – Raeder repeating Keitel's directive for "heavy blows struck by surprise" – Denmark, Norway, Belgium, Holland, Russia. As Hitler had said in the presence of a number of these men: "Considerations of right or wrong or treaties do not enter into the matter." ...

'Every one of these men knew of these plans at one stage or another in their development. Every one of these men acquiesced in this technique, knowing full well what it must represent in terms of human life. How can any one of them now say he was not a party to common murder in its most ruthless form?'

Shawcross again addressed Jahrreiss's legal arguments. But the real point was that the defendants were common murders. To reinforce the point he reread the testimony of Hermann Gräbe on the massacre of local Jews he had witnessed in the Ukraine:

## CHAPTER FIFTEEN

*During the fifteen minutes I stood near, I heard no complaint or plea for mercy. I watched a family of about eight persons, a man and a woman both of about fifty, with their children of about twenty to twenty-four, and two grown-up daughters about twenty-eight or twenty-nine. An old woman with snow-white hair was holding a one-year-old child in her arms and singing to it and tickling it. The child was cooing with delight. The parents were looking on with tears in their eyes. The father was holding the hand of a boy about ten years old and speaking to him softly; the boy was fighting his tears. The father pointed to the sky, stroked his head and seemed to explain something to him ....*

Rebecca West recorded that, at this point, 'all the defendants wriggled on their seats, like children rated at by a schoolmaster, while their faces grew old'.

'In one way the fate of these men means little: their personal power for evil lies for ever broken; they have convicted and discredited each other and finally destroyed the legend they created round the figure of their leader,' said Shawcross. 'But on their fate great issues must still depend, for the ways of truth and righteousness between the nations of the world, the hope of future international co-operation in the administration of law and justice are in your hands. This trial must form a milestone in the history of civilization, not only bringing retribution to these guilty men, not only marking that right shall in the end triumph over evil, but also that the ordinary people of the world – and I make no distinction now between friend and foe – are now determined that the individual must transcend the state.'

Not to be outdone by Jackson quoting Shakespeare, Shawcross added a few words from Goethe.

He concluded: 'You will remember when you come to give your decision the story of Gräbe, but not in vengeance – in a determination that these things shall not occur again. The father – do you remember? – pointed to the sky, and seemed to say something to his boy.'

*As the German Army pushed deep into the Soviet Union, Einsatzgruppen – death squads – went in behind them to kill Soviet officials and Jews.*

# Chapter Sixteen
# Illegal Organizations

Once the closing arguments for the defence and prosecution were over, it was time to hear the case for the defence of the six organizations also indicted – the leadership corps of the Nazi Party, the Reich cabinet, the SS, the SD, the SA and the general staff and high command of the German armed forces.

According to the rules of procedure adopted on 29 October 1945, the tribunal was to appeal to members of these organizations, telling them that they were 'entitled to apply to the tribunal for leave to be heard'. However, 'nothing herein contained shall be construed to confer immunity of any kind upon such members of said groups or organizations'.

As a result, notices had been put in newspapers, flyers had been handed out and appeals had been broadcast. By April 1946, more than 300,000 affidavits had been taken. No fewer than 3,000 documents were submitted and 200 witnesses stood ready, even though it had proved difficult to get co-operation from the Soviet zone, particularly from the prisoner of war camps there.

Plainly this was going to cause difficulties – and not just because of the sheer quantity of evidence. Declaring these organizations illegal meant hundreds of thousands of Germans became criminals overnight. There had been more than 4.5 million members of the SA. Hundreds of thousands had been in the SS, while between 600,000 and 700,000 had been in the leadership corps of the Nazi Party.

## Illegal Organizations

Searching to reassure the lowliest member, Robert Jackson said: 'The United States is not interested in coming over here 3,500 miles to prosecute clerks and stenographers and janitors.'

### The Nazi Party
The first on trial was the leadership corps of the Nazi Party, defended by Dr Robert Servatius. He called witnesses to show that the lowest Party officials, the blockleiters, collected money to support the Nazi Party, perpetrated some of the violence on Kristallnacht and contributed to the suppression of the trades unions. Some were simply busybodies and low-level informants, hardly war criminals.

Defending the Gestapo and the SD, Rudolf Merkel pointed out that there were numerous telephone operators and typists in these organizations. However, in the testimony already given to the court, there was a great deal of evidence to show that both organizations participated in the torture and murder of political opponents, hostages and captured Allied combatants. Witnesses were keen to blame the SS, but the SD and Gestapo – who trained together and often wore the same uniforms – were jointly administered with the SS after 1939.

### The Reich cabinet
There was little point in including the Reich cabinet on the indictment. It had not met since 1937 and, during the entire period of Nazi rule, only 48 men had held cabinet rank: 17 of them were in the dock anyway; the missing Bormann was another member; and a further eight were thought to be dead. However, the Americans particularly wanted to show that Nazi institutions as well as individuals were criminal.

Only one defence witness was called: former minister of justice, Dr Walter Schellenberg, who pointed out that cabinet members were forbidden to resign. However, two had stepped down and although most of their tasks were performed by functionaries appointed by Hitler, draft laws and budgets were circulated so members were aware of Hitler's policies.

## The SS

Witnesses called to defend the SS claimed that it was made up of small independent units that knew little of what the others were doing. The only common factor was their overall command by Heinrich Himmler. The crimes, it seems, were carried out by individuals who just happened to be wearing SS uniforms.

However, when the manager of the German Ancestral Heritage Institute, Wolfram Sievers, came to the stand, he admitted under cross-examination to having corresponded with the SS at Auschwitz, the Reich security main office and various other SS officials when collecting the skulls of 'Jewish-Bolshevik commissars' for his collection. This showed that there was no overall structure to the organization; it also entered into testimony more hideous details of experiments being carried out on concentration-camp inmates.

The defence suffered another setback when it called two SS judges. SS Judge Reinecke claimed that individual violations of international law did occur – 'these were isolated occurrences and not systematic. All these individual acts were prosecuted under the jurisdiction of the SS and the police in the most severe manner.'

The conditions in the concentration camps in the film screened in court merely showed 'the effect of the total collapse of the German Reich on the concentration camps; it does not, therefore, represent normal conditions in such camps,' he maintained.

SS Judge Morgen described the conditions at Buchenwald, which he had visited repeatedly, listing its facilities – a wonderful view, lawns and flowerbeds, a huge library, regular mail service, a cinema, admirable sports facilities and a brothel. Everyone in the courtroom burst out laughing. Lawrence, who seems to have been dozing, asked Biddle what the witness had said. Biddle's stomach seems to have brushed against the switch, turning his microphone on, and he was heard to reply:

'Brothel, Geoffrey, brothel.'

'What?' said Lawrence, taken aback.

'Bordello, brothel, whorehouse,' said Biddle.

More laughter.

There was further levity when Baron von Eberstein said that he felt that it was his duty and 'in keeping with the tradition of his family' to join the SS along with four princes and an archbishop. The suggestion that they could all have been Rhodes scholars reduced Maxwell Fyfe to fits of giggles.

## *The Waffen-SS*

The defence tried to distance the fighting units of the Waffen-SS from the doings of the organization as a whole. As the war progressed, it came under the overall command of the Wehrmacht and was increasingly filled with conscripts.

They called Paul Hausser, a general in the Waffen-SS, who claimed it was a 'fourth branch of the Army'.

'Our method of fighting was supervised and ordered by the Army, and ... we did not gain prestige through cruel methods,' he said. 'The commanders who had personal pride in leading a clean fighting unit against the enemy saw to that. I learned only here of the participation of small units of the Waffen-SS in the evacuation of the Warsaw ghetto or in the executions which took place in Bohemia and Moravia.'

## CHAPTER SIXTEEN

Asked about the killing of prisoners, he said: 'These incidents are not the result of training, but rather the failure of individuals, perhaps the giving way of nerves when in difficult situations deep in enemy territory.'

Further cross-examination showed that the Waffen-SS had co-operated with the Einsatzgruppen, had shot hostages and had guarded concentration camps. Waffen-SS units were addressed by Himmler on the need for terror. It was clearly not a distinct organization.

### General staff and high command

On 9 August the defence for the general staff and high command was heard. The British were dubious about this prosecution, but the Americans were insistent. They thought it a vital component in showing that there was a conspiracy to wage an aggressive war; it did not seem right, they argued, that junior members of the armed forces should be prosecuted, while those above them went free.

The first witness for the defence was Field Marshal Walther von Brauchitsch, Commander-in-Chief of the Germany Army from 1938 to 1941. He said that he had not known beforehand of plans to occupy Austria, the Sudetenland or the rest of Czechoslovakia. The orders had come direct from Hitler. He had advised against any action against Poland, fearing it would cause war, and there had been no plans to attack in the West until Hitler ordered it.

'In the case of Russia, we were concerned with the fact that if a war were to break out at all, it was to be a preventive war,' said von Brauchitsch. 'In the conference I limited myself to the purely military misgivings.'

But Hitler did not listen. After he failed to take Moscow in the winter of 1940, von Brauchitsch was sacked. He also claimed to have known nothing about military agreements with Japan. Indeed, his entire testimony was a string of

## Illegal Organizations

denials. Facing charges himself, he died in October 1948 before standing trial for war crimes.

Field Marshal Erich von Manstein, who devised the plan of attack on France, claimed that the general staff was held at arm's length from Hitler.

'As far as the high command of the armed forces is concerned, if it had a will of its own at all, it did not, in my opinion, have the possibility seriously to express that will in opposition to Hitler,' he said.

In 1949, von Manstein went on trial on 17 charges that included the maltreatment of prisoners of war, co-operation with the Einsatzgruppe D in killing Jewish residents of the Crimea, and disregarding the welfare of civilians by using scorched-earth tactics while retreating from the Soviet Union. He was convicted on nine charges. Sentenced to 18 years in prison, he was released in 1953.

Field Marshal Gerd von Rundstedt, who had held command on both the Eastern and Western Fronts, said that the generals did not discuss politics, quoting British Field Marshal Bernard Montgomery: 'As a servant of the nation, the Army is above politics, and that must remain so.'

Again von Rundstedt claimed to have had no prior knowledge of Hitler's plans of attack, learning of them only through official channels. He and his fellow officers had opposed the Commissar and Commando orders and sought to make them ineffective. He also claimed that Hitler did not heed the advice of his generals.

In 1948, von Rundstedt was charged with 'the maltreatment and killing of civilians and prisoners of war ... killing hostages, illegal employment of prisoners of war, deportation of forced labour to Germany ... mass execution of Jews ... and other war crimes, yet to be specified'. However, he was judged unfit to stand trial. He was released in May 1949 and died in February 1953.

## CHAPTER SIXTEEN

*Field Marshal Gerd von Rundstedt viewed Hitler with aristocratic disdain, but refused to participate in any plot to get rid of him.*

## Illegal Organizations

The final organization to be given its defence was the SA, but it had ceased to be a cohesive organization after the purge in 1934. It had had so little influence that the case against it was poorly documented.

Dodd summed up: 'It is a strange feature of this trial that counsel for the respective organizations have not sought to deny these crimes but only to shift responsibility for their commission. The military defendants blame the political leaders for initiating wars of aggression; the Gestapo blames the soldiers for the murder of escaped prisoners of war; the SA blames the Gestapo for concentration camp murders; the Gestapo blames the leadership corps for anti-Jewish pogroms; the SS blames the cabinet for the concentration camp system; and the cabinet blames the SS for the exterminations in the East.'

## Chapter Seventeen
# Final Statements

On 31 August, the defendants were permitted to give short speeches, which were to be their final statements to the German people. Göring said: 'I wish to state expressly that I condemn these terrible mass murders to the utmost, and cannot understand them in the least. But I should like to state clearly once more before the high tribunal that I have never decreed the murder of a single individual at any time, and neither did I decree any other atrocities or tolerate them, while I had the power and the knowledge to prevent them....

'I did not want a war, nor did I bring it about. I did everything to prevent it by negotiations. After it had broken out, I did everything to assure victory. Since the three greatest powers on Earth, together with many other nations, were fighting against us, we finally succumbed to their tremendous superiority. I stand up for the things that I have done, but I deny most emphatically that my actions were dictated by the desire to subjugate foreign peoples by wars, to murder them, to rob them, or to enslave them, or to commit atrocities or crimes.'

Later, at lunch, von Papen asked him simply: 'Who in the world is responsible for all this destruction if not you?'

Everyone was surprised that Hess wanted to speak. He had a five-page statement that he read seated. It was rambling and incoherent. Lawrence cut him short, insisting that these final pleas should last for no more than 20 minutes. Hess concluded: 'I was permitted to work for many years of my life under the greatest son whom my people has brought forth in its thousand-year history. Even if I could, I would not want to erase this period of time from my existence. I am happy to know that I have done my duty, to my people, my duty as a German, as a National Socialist, as a loyal follower of my Führer. I do not regret anything.'

Ribbentrop did his case little good when he read a telegram from Stalin received in 1939 after the invasion of Poland, saying: 'The friendship of Germany and the Soviet Union, based on the blood which they have shed together, has every prospect of being a firm and lasting one.'

Keitel said: 'I believed, but I erred, and I was not in a position to prevent what ought to have been prevented. That is my guilt.'

Kaltenbrunner complained: 'I am accused here because substitutes are needed for the missing Himmler ....'

Rosenberg claimed that he had done 'honest service' for his ideology and said: 'I understood my struggle, just as the struggle of many thousands of my comrades, to be one conducted for the noblest idea.'

Frank regretted that Hitler left no final statement – 'Amid the deepest distress of his people, he found no comforting word.'

Frick insisted that he had a clear conscience. 'My entire life was spent in the service of my people and my fatherland,' he said.

Streicher said that in *Der Stürmer* he had advocated Zionism. 'I did not want the Jewish problem to be solved by violence.'

In tears, Funk admitted that he had made many mistakes. 'I, too, have let myself be deceived in many things and I frankly acknowledge ... that I have let myself be deceived

## CHAPTER SEVENTEEN

all too easily, and in many ways have been too unconcerened and too gullible. Therein I see my guilt ...' he said.

'To be sure, I erred politically,' said Schacht. 'I never claimed to be a politician .... My political mistake was not realizing the extent of Hitler's criminal nature at an early enough time. But I did not stain my hands with one single illegal or immoral act.'

Dönitz maintained his justification of submarine warfare and stuck up for the Führer principle that brought 'a feeling of happiness such as the entire nation had never known before'. However, in retrospect the Führerprinzip must be wrong 'because apparently human nature is not in a position to use the power of this principle for good, without falling victim to the temptations of this power'.

Raeder said: 'I have done my duty as a soldier because it was my conviction that this was the best way for me to serve the German people and fatherland, for which I have lived and for which I am prepared to die at any moment.'

Schirach made an appeal on behalf of German youth – that it 'be declared free of guilt. Joyfully it will grasp the hand which is stretched out to it across the ruins and debris,' he said.

Sauckel also cried when he said: 'I have been shaken to the very depths of my soul by the atrocities revealed in this trial ... I dedicated myself to socialist love and justice toward those whose only wealth is their labour and, at the same time, to the destiny of my nation.'

Jodl, too, was unrepentant, saying: 'I believe and avow that a man's duty toward his people and fatherland stands above every other. To carry out this duty was for me an honour, and the highest law. May this duty be supplanted in some happier future by an even higher one, by the duty toward humanity.'

## Final Statements

'When I examine my conscience,' said von Papen, 'I do not find any guilt where the Prosecution has looked for it and claims to have found it. But where is the man without guilt and without faults?' He explained: 'The power of evil was stronger than the power of good and drove Germany inevitably into catastrophe.'

To Seyss-Inquart, Hitler was still the messiah: 'To me he remains the man who made Greater Germany a fact in German history. I served this man. And now? I cannot today cry "Crucify him," since yesterday I cried "Hosanna."'

Speer sounded a warning against the dangers posed by the weapons developed during the war. 'In five or ten years the technique of warfare will make it possible to fire rockets from continent to continent with uncanny precision. By atomic power it can destroy one million people in the centre of New York in a matter of seconds with a rocket operated, perhaps, by only ten men, invisible, without previous warning, faster than sound, by day and by night.'

Von Neurath claimed to have 'a clear conscience not only before myself, but before history and the German people'. But were he to be found guilty, he would 'take it upon myself as a last sacrifice on behalf of my people'.

After 216 days of testimony, the tribunal was adjourned to consider its judgement. It would take a month.

## Chapter Eighteen
# The Judgement

On 1 October 1946, the verdict was handed down. Hans Frank, the governor-general of Poland; Wilhelm Frick, minister of internal affairs; Alfred Jodl, Hitler's strategic adviser; Ernst Kaltenbrunner, head of the RSHA; Field Marshal Wilhelm Keitel; Joachim von Ribbentrop, Hitler's foreign minister; Alfred Rosenberg, minister for the occupied territories; Fritz Sauckel, organizer of forced labour; Julius Streicher, anti-Semitic propagandist and Gauleiter in Franconia; and Arthur Seyss-Inquart, commissioner for the occupied Netherlands, were all sentenced to death and hanged in the early morning of 16 October 1946 in the old gymnasium of the Nuremberg prison. The bodies were cremated in Munich and the ashes were strewn in an estuary of the Isar River.

The head of the Luftwaffe, Hermann Göring, was also sentenced to death, but committed suicide before he could be executed. And Nazi party organizer Martin Bormann was sentenced to death *in absentia*, though he was officially declared dead in 1973 after a body identified as his had been unearthed in Berlin.

Walther Funk, minister for economic affairs and president of the German central bank, was sentenced to life imprisonment, but was released in 1957 due to illness. He died in 1960. Erich Raeder, Commander-in-Chief of the German Navy, got life, but was released in 1955 due to illness and died in 1960. Rudolf Hess was also sentenced

## The Judgement

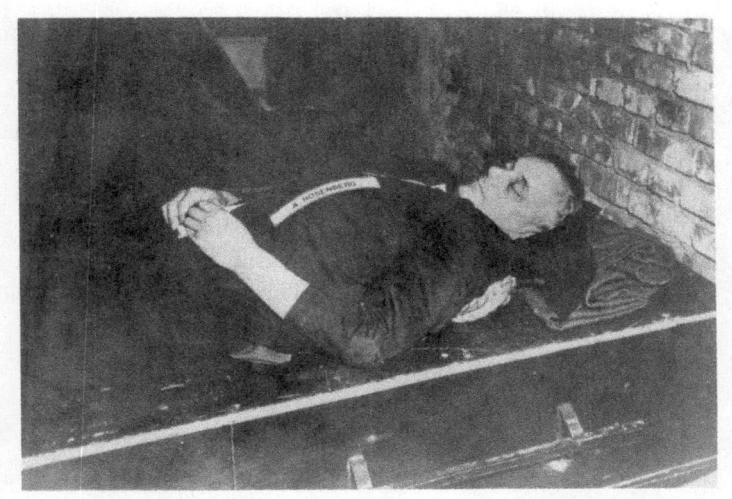

*Alfred Rosenberg was the ideologist of Nazism and minister for the occupied territories. He was found guilty and hanged.*

to life imprisonment. He committed suicide in 1987 in Spandau prison in Berlin, where the other Nuremberg detainees had been held.

Karl Dönitz, Admiral of the Fleet and Hitler's successor, was sentenced to ten years' imprisonment. He was released in 1956 and died in 1980. Albert Speer, minister for weapons and munitions, was sentenced to 20 years. Released in 1966, he died in 1981. Baldur von Schirach, head of the ministry for youth and Gauleiter of Vienna, was also sentenced to 20 years. He was released in 1966 and died in 1974. And Konstantin von Neurath, Protector of Bohemia and Moravia, was sentenced to 15 years' imprisonment. Released in 1954 due to illness, he died in 1956.

Hans Fritzsche, head of the news service section in the ministry of propaganda and essentially a stand-in for Goebbels, who had committed suicide, was acquitted, but

## CHAPTER EIGHTEEN

in the subsequent denazification procedures a German court sentenced him to nine years' imprisonment. He was released in 1950 and died in 1953. Franz von Papen, vice-chancellor in Hitler's first cabinet, was also acquitted. In denazification procedures, he was sentenced to eight years' imprisonment. Released in 1949, he died in 1969. Also acquitted was Hjalmar Schacht, president of the Reichsbank and minister of economics who had been imprisoned in the concentration camp at Flossenbürg since 1944. The German authorities imprisoned him until 1948. He died in 1970.

Guilty verdicts were also handed down on the leadership corps of the NSDAP, the SS, the SD and the Gestapo.

# Epilogue

Although it was originally planned for the International Military Tribunal to sit again, the Cold War had started and there was no further co-operation among the participants. However, further military tribunals sat in the separate French, British, American and Soviet zones of occupation. The US tribunals sat at Nuremberg and on 9 December 1946, proceedings began against 23 German doctors accused of participating in the Nazi euthanasia programme to murder the mentally deficient and of conducting medical experiments on concentration camp inmates. The trial lasted 140 days: 85 witnesses appeared and 1,500 documents were introduced in evidence; 16 of the doctors were found guilty. Seven were sentenced to death and executed on 2 June 1948.

In the 12 subsequent proceedings at Nuremberg, 175 Germans were convicted. In all, 10,000 Germans were convicted and 250 sentenced to death.

In 1960 Adolf Eichmann was found in Argentina. He was kidnapped by the Israeli intelligence agency Mossad and taken to Israel to stand trial. He was convicted and hanged two years later. Josef Mengele was also found in South America. Escaping capture, he died of a stroke while swimming in 1979; he was only identified later by his dental records.

### *Japanese war trials*
The Potsdam Declaration of July 1945 called for trial of those who had 'deceived and misled' the Japanese people

# EPILOGUE

into war. As commander of the occupation, General Douglas MacArthur arrested 39 suspects, most of them members of General Tojo's war cabinet. Tojo himself tried to commit suicide, but was resuscitated by American doctors.

In Manila, MacArthur had already held war crimes trials that had resulted in the executions of generals Yamashita and Homma and there were doubts about the legitimacy of such proceedings. Nevertheless, on 6 October MacArthur was given the authority to try suspects under three broad categories. Class A charges alleging 'crimes against peace' were to be brought against Japan's top leaders who had planned and directed the war. Class B and C charges, which could be levelled at Japanese of any rank, covered 'conventional war crimes' and 'crimes against humanity' respectively. And in early November, MacArthur was also given authority to purge other wartime leaders from public life.

On 19 January 1946, the International Military Tribunal for the Far East was established with 11 judges. Sir William Webb, an Australian, was the tribunal's president and US assistant attorney general Joseph Keenan was named chief prosecutor.

The Tokyo trials began on 3 May 1946, and lasted two and a half years. By 4 November 1948, all of the remaining defendants had been found guilty. Seven were sentenced to death, 16 to life terms and two to lesser terms. Two had died during the trials and one had been found insane. After reviewing their decisions, MacArthur praised the work of the tribunal and upheld the verdicts.

On 23 December 1948, General Tojo and six others were hanged at Sugamo prison. Afraid of antagonizing the Japanese people, MacArthur defied the wishes of President Truman and banned photography. Instead four members of the Allied Council were present as official witnesses.

The Tokyo trials were not the only forum for the punishment of Japanese war criminals. The Asian countries that had suffered under the Japanese war machine tried an estimated 5,000 suspected war criminals, executing as many as 900 and sentencing more than half to life in prison.

# Index

*Italic figures denote illustrations.*

Ahrens, Friedrich 150
Albrecht, Ralph 37–8
Alderman, Sidney
  presents evidence at prosecution opening 38
  statement on waging aggressive war 44
Amen, Colonel 109, 111
Amery, John 25
Andrus, Burton C. 22
  on Walther Funk 58
  stops Hermann Göring reading 102
*Atrocities of the German Fascist Invaders in the USSR, The* 77
Babel, Ludwig 51
Babi Yar massacre 76
Bach-Zelewski, Erich von dem 54–5
Balachowsky, Alfred 71
Bergold, Friedrich 149
Bernays, Murray 14–15
Biddle, Francis B.
  on tribunal 24, 25
  protects defence counsels 27–8
  chastises Sam Harris 48
  and Robert Storey's evidence 48
  on Erich von dem Bach-Zelewski 55
  reaction to evidence from Soviet prosecutors 76
  rules Alfred Seidel's evidence inadmissible 98
  and Fritz Sauckel's testimony 132
  and Judge Morgen's testimony 169
Birkett, Sir Norman 23
  on tribunal 24, 25
  on Egon Kubuschok 27
  chastises Sam Harris 48
  on evidence about torture 72
  reaction to evidence from Soviet prosecutors 76
  on Hermann Göring's testimony 92
  on Hjalmar Schacht's testimony 122
Blaha, Franz 59–62
Blank, Margarete 101
Bodenschatz, Karl 85–6
Bohle, Ernst 98
Bormann, Martin 20, *21*, 62, 149, 158, 178
Bracchtl, Dr 61
Brauchitsch, Bernd von 87
Brauchitsch, Walther von 170–71
Briande, Aristide 64
Brudno, Walter W. 56–7
Canaris, Admiral 40, 41, 105
Cappelen, Hans 72
Churchill, Winston
  calls for retribution against Germany 11
  initial support for shooting Nazi leaders 12
  and 'Statement on Atrocities' 12

# INDEX

at Tehran Conference 13–14, *13*
'Iron Curtain' speech 83–4, 91
Ciano, Gian Galeazzo 102, 135–6
Clark, Andrew 26–7
concentrations camps
  films on shown 39
  evidence on 47–8, 80
  testimony of Franz Blaha 59–62
  testimony of Maurice Lampe 68–9
  testimony of Marie-Claude Vaillant-Couturier 69–71
  testimony of Victor Dupont 71–2
  testimony of Abraham Stzkever 80
  testimony of Samuel Rajzman 80–82
  testimony of Jacob Vernik 82–3
  Hermann Göring questioned on 92, 95
  Joachim von Ribbentrop questioned on 103
  Ernst Kaltenbrenner questioned on 108–9
  testimony of Rudolf Höss 108, 111–12
  testimony of Arthur Seyss-Inquart 136
  testimony of Judge Reinecke 168
  testimony of Judge Morgen 169
Dahlerus, Birger 89–90, 95
*Daily Express* 92
*Daily Herald* 76
*Daily Telegraph* 95, 101, 102
Debenest, Delphin 136
defence counsels 26–8
  and access to briefs 38
*Der Stürmer* 58, 116, 117, 175
Dix, Rudolf 27
Dodd, Thomas
  presents evidence on forced labour 45–7
  presents evidence on concentration camps 47

questions Alfred Rosenberg 112
questions Walther Funk 123–4
questions Baldur von Schirach 130
Dollfuss, Engelbert 138, 145
Dönitz, Karl 19
  defence counsel for 27
  during prosecution opening 31
  reaction to film of concentration camp 39
  visited by prison psychiatrist 40
  during Robert Storey's presentation 49
  evidence against 62–3
  denies knowledge of concentration camps 80
  gives testimony 125–7
  in Robert Jackson's closing statement 157
  final statement of 176
  sentenced to imprisonment 179
Dos Passos, John 29
Dupont, Victor 71–2
Eberstein, Baron von 169
Eichborn, Reinhard von 150
Eichmann, Adolf 17, 47, 53–4, 183
Einsatzgruppen 49–51, *165*
Epaux, Annette 70
Ernst, Karl 93
Fagence, Maurice 76–7
Falco, Robert 24, 25
Farr, Warren 49
Faure, Edgar 103
First World War
  war trials after 9–11
Flachsner, Hans 141
forced labour, *142*
  evidence on 45–7, 65
  in Soviet Union 79–80
  Hermann Göring's knowledge of 95
  testimony of Fritz Sauckel 131–3
  testimony of Albert Speer 140, 141–3

# INDEX

Frank, Hans 19, 22, *57*
  defence counsel for 26
  as possible defence counsel 27
  during prosecution opening 31
  in opening statement for
    prosecution 34, 36
  visited by prison psychiatrist 40
  in evidence on forced labour 46
  evidence against 57–8
  gives testimony 113
  in Robert Jackson's closing
    statement 156
  final statement of 176
Freisler, Roland 45, *45*
Frick, Wilhelm 19, *57*, *115*, *135*
  during prosecution opening 31
  testimony of Franz Blaha 62
  defence witnesses for 113–14
  in Robert Jackson's closing
    statement 156–7
  final statement of 175
  sentenced to death 178
Fritzsche, Hans 23, 49, 116
  on Sir Geoffrey Lawrence 23
  during prosecution opening 31
  visited by prison psychiatrist 40
  evidence against 147–9
  gives testimony 148–9
  in Robert Jackson's closing
    statement 158
  acquitted 179–80
Funk, Walther 20, *135*
  during prosecution opening 31, 32
  evidence against 58
  testimony of Franz Blaha 62
  gives testimony 122–3
  in Robert Jackson's closing
    statement 157
  final statement of 175
  sentenced to imprisonment
    178
general staff and high command
  testimony of Erich von dem
    Bach-Zelewski 54–5
  defence counsel for 170–71
Germanization
  evidence of 48
Gestapo
  on trial 22
  evidence on by Robert Storey 49
  defence counsel for 167
  found guilty 180
Gigoriev, Jacob 79
Gilbert, Gustav 39–40
  questions Erwin Lahousen 41
  and Hess' sanity 42
Gisevius, Hans Bernd 114–15, 119
Goebbels, Joseph 17, 56, 93, 147, 148
Göring, Hermann *18*, *90*
  in captivity 17–18
  on Sir Geoffrey Lawrence 24
  chooses Otto Stahmer as defence
    counsel 26
  during prosecution opening 31, 32, 33, 37
  pleas not guilty 33
  in opening statement for
    prosecution 35, 36
  reaction to film of concentration
    camp 39
  visited by prison psychiatrist
    39–40
  and Erwin Lahousen's evidence 41
  reacts to films on Nazi Plan 44
  on Erich von dem Bach-Zelewski 55
  on Friedrich Paulus 75
  denies knowledge of concentration
    camps 80
  reaction to Churchill's 'Iron
    Curtain' speech 84, 85
  as lead for the defence 85
  defence witnesses for 85–90
  gives testimony 90–6
  questioned by Robert Jackson 93–5
  argues with Joachim von
    Ribbentrop 102

# INDEX

on Wilhelm Keitel 103
testimony of Hans Bernd
   Gisevius 114–15
and Night of the Long Knives
   138
in Robert Jackson's closing
   statement 154, 156
final statement of 174
commits suicide 178
Gräbe, Hermann 49–51, 163–4
'Great Escape' shootings 92, 95, 107
Griffith-Jones, J.M.G. 117
Halbach, Krupp von Bohlen und 20
Harris, Sam 48
Hausser, Paul 169–70
Herzog, Jacques B.
  presents evidence on forced
   labour 65
  questions Fritz Sauckel 131–2
Hess, Rudolf 19, *57*, *97*
  defence counsel for 28
  during prosecution opening 31,
   33, 37
  in opening statement for
   prosecution 37
  reaction to film of concentration
   camp 39
  declared legally sane 41–2
  reaction to Churchill's 'Iron
   Curtain' speech 84
  prosecution evidence against
   97–9
  in Robert Jackson's closing
   statement 156
  final statement of 174–5
  sentenced to imprisonment 178–9
Himmler, Heinrich 17, 47, 58, 169
Hindenburg, Paul von 10
Hitler, Adolf
  racial beliefs 11
  plans for at the end of war 12
  commits suicide 17
  in opening statement for
   prosecution 35
  and 'Night and Fog'
   disappearances 66, 67
  and Göring's testimony 91
  Hermann Göring's loyalty to 96
  and Rudolf Hess 98–9
  and Joachim von Ribbentrop's
   defence 101
  Wilhelm Keitel's view of 104–5
  Hjalmar Schacht's view of 118–19
  and Albert Speer's testimony
   140–41
  and Konstantin Von Neurath's
   testimony 143–4
Hitler Youth 128–31, *129*
Horn, Martin 99, 100
Horthy, Admiral 96
Höss, Rudolf 109, 111–12
illegal seizures
  evidence of 65–6, 77–78
Institute for the Exploration of the
  Jewish Question 56
International Military Tribunal 16
*Izvestia* 128
Jackson, Robert H. 43
  opening statement for prosecution
   7–8, 36–9
  appointed as chief United States
   prosecutor 15
  and London Charter 15
  on prosecution team 25
  questions Erwin Lahousen 40–41
  leads prosecution of Nazi Party 83
  questions Karl Bodenschatz 85–6
  questions Hermann Göring 93–5
  refuses Alfred Rosenberg's
   request for documents 112
  questions Hjalmar Schacht 120–22
  questions Albert Speer 141–2
  closing statement of 153–61
Jaeger, Wilhelm 132
Jahrreiss, Hermann 153
Japanese war trials 181–3
Jewish persecution
  evidence on 48

# INDEX

and Alfred Rosenberg 56–7
evidence from Soviet prosecution 79
testimony of Samuel Rajzman 80–82
testimony of Jacob Vernik 82–3
Hermann Göring's knowledge of 96
Ribbentrop questioned on 103
testimony of Hans Frank 112
testimony of Julius Streicher 116–17
testimony of Arthur Seyss-Inquart 136
Jodl, Alfred 20, 117
during prosecution opening 38
visited by prison psychiatrist 40
in Erwin Lahousen's evidence 41
give testimony 133–4
in Robert Jackson's closing statement 157
final statement of 174
sentenced to death 178
Jost, Heinz *52*
Joyce, William 25
Kaltenbrunner, Ernst 19
and prosecution opening 31
joins defendants 47
testimony of Otto Ohlendorf 51–3
testimony of Franz Blaha 62
gives testimony 108–09
testimony of Rudolf Höss 109, 111–12
in Robert Jackson's closing statement 157
final statement of 175
sentenced to death 178
Katyn Forest massacre 13, 76, 149–51, *151*
Kaufmann, Kurt 43, 107, 146
Keenan, Joseph 182
Keitel, Wilhelm 20, *106*
defence counsel for 26
during prosecution opening 31
in opening statement for prosecution 35, 36
visited by prison psychiatrist 40
in Erwin Lahousen's evidence 40, 41
and Telford Taylor's evidence 54
and 'Night and Fog' disappearances 67–8
gives testimony 103–7
in Robert Jackson's closing statement 156
final statement of 175
sentenced to death 178
Kellogg, Frank B. 64
Kellogg-Briand Pact 43, 64, 153
Kesselring, Albert 87–9, *88*
Koch, Erich 46
Koch, Ilse 47–8
Koch, Karl 47
Kramer, Josef 27
Kranzbühler, Otto 27, 80
Krupp, Alfried 26–7
Kuboschok, Egon 27
Lahousen, Erwin 40–41
Lammers, Hans 107
Lampe, Maurice 68–9
*Last Attempt, The* (Dahlerus) 89
Lawrence, Sir Geoffrey 24, 152
opens Nuremberg Trials 6
on tribunal *23*, 23–4, 25
during prosecution opening 32–3
ensures evidence given to defence counsels 38–9
reaction to film of concentration camp 39
and Rudolf Hess' sanity 42
and Robert Storey's evidence 48
and questioning of Hermann Göring 94
and Joachim von Ribbentrop's testimony 102
and Julius Streicher's testimony 117
and Judge Morgen's testimony 169

# INDEX

and Rudolf Hess' final statement 174–5
Ley, Robert 20, 77–8
London Charter 15–16, 28, 31, 43
looting
  evidence on 65
MacArthur, Douglas 182
Malmedy massacre 14
*Manchester Guardian* 125
Manstein, Erich von 171
Marx, Hanns 116, 117
Maxwell Fyfe, Sir David
  on prosecution team 25
  helps Hermann Göring with defence counsel 26
  statement on waging aggressive war 44
  questions Albert Kesselring 87–89
  questions Birger Dahlerus 89
  questions Hermann Göring 95–6
  presents evidence against Rudolf Hess 98–9
  questions Joachim von Ribbentrop's interpreter 101
  questions Joachim von Ribbentrop 102–3
  questions Wilhelm Keitel 105, 107
  and Julius Streicher's testimony 118
  questions Erich Raeder 127–8
  questions Franz Von Papen 139–41
  questions Konstantin Von Neurath 144–7
  on leadership system in Third Reich 153
  and Baron von Eberstein's testimony 169
*Mein Kampf* (Hitler) 98, 118
Mengele, Josef 17, 181
Menthon, François de 25–6
Merkel, Rudolf 167

Milch, Erhard 86–7
Morgen, Judge 169
Morgenthau, Henry 14
Moyland, Gustav Steengracht von 100–01
*Myth of the Twentieth Century, The* (Rosenberg) 56
Nazi Party
  leadership on trial 20
  evidence on by Robert Storey 48–9
  prosecution evidence against 82, 167
  found guilty 180
Nazi Plan
  films on shown 44–5
Neave, Airey 28
Nelte, Otto
  and Erwin Lahousen's evidence 41
  questions Friedrich Paulus 75
Neurath, Konstantin von 19, *135*
  during prosecution opening 31
  in opening statement for prosecution 35
  visited by prison psychiatrist 40
  evidence against 63
  gives testimony 143–7
  in Robert Jackson's closing statement 158
  final statement of 177
  sentenced to imprisonment 179
*New York Times* 107, 120, 122
'Night and Fog' disappearances 66–8, 104
Night of the Long Knives 49, 55, 114–15, 118, 138, 145
Nikitchenko, Iona Timofeevich 16, 23, 24, 25
Nimitz, Chester 127
Nuremberg Trials
  opened by Sir Geoffrey Lawrence 6
  lead up to 11–16
  plans for 14

# INDEX

London Charter 15–16
  venue decided 16
  security at 22, 30
  membership of tribunal 23–5
  prosecution team 25–6
  defence counsels 26–8
  simultaneous translation at 28–9
  press at 29
Oberhauser, Eugen 150–51
Ohlendorf, Otto 51–3, *52*
Pannenberg, Otto 114
Papen, Franz von 20, *57*, *135*
  Egon Kubuschok as defence counsel 27
  during prosecution opening 31
  reaction to film of concentration camp 39
  evidence against 63
  gives testimony 138–40
  in Robert Jackson's closing statement 157–8
  final statement of 176–9
  acquitted 180
Parker, John J.
  on tribunal 24, 25
  during prosecution opening 32–3
  reaction to evidence from Soviet prosecutors 76–7
Paulus, Friedrich 74–5
Potsdam Declaration 181–2
prisoners of war
  evidence of treatment of 68–9, 75–6
  Göring denies knowledge of ill-treatment 92
prosecution team 25–6
Puhl, Emil 125
Raeder, Erich 20
  during prosecution opening 31
  in opening statement for prosecution 35
  evidence against 63
  give testimony 127–8
  in Robert Jackson's closing statement 157
  final statement of 176
  sentenced to imprisonment 178
Rajzman, Samuel 80–82
Rascher, Sigmund 60, 61
Reich cabinet
  on trial 20
  Egon Kubuschok as defence counsel 27
  evidence against 167–8
Reinecke, Judge 168
Ribbentrop, Joachim von 19, *100*
  defence counsel for 26
  during prosecution opening 31, 32
  in opening statement for prosecution 35
  reaction to film of concentration camp 39
  in Erwin Lahousen's evidence 41
  evidence against 63, 99
  in Birger Dahlerus' testimony 89–90
  in Hermann Göring's testimony 95
  defence witnesses for 100–01
  gives testimony 101–3
  in Robert Jackson's closing statement 156, 160
  final statement of 175
  sentenced to death 178
Roberts, G.D. 'Khaki' 133–4
Röhm, Ernst 49, 93, 114
Roosevelt, Franklin D.
  calls for retribution against Germany 11
  at Tehran Conference 13, *13*, 14
  view of war trials 15
Rosenberg, Alfred 19, *57*, 178, *179*
  defence counsel for 26, 27
  during prosecution opening 31
  in opening statement for prosecution 36
  and theft of works of art 48
  evidence against 56–7

# INDEX

gives testimony 112–13
in Robert Jackson's closing
    statement 156, 160
final statement of 175
sentenced to death 178
Rudenko, Roman Andreyovich
    on prosecution team 26
    tries to delay start of trial 31
    opening statement on war crimes
        in the East 73–4
    questions Hermann Göring 96
    questions Hans Fritzsche 149
Rundstedt, Gerd von 171, *172*
SA
    on trial 22, 173
    evidence on by Robert Storey 49
Sauckel, Fritz 19–20, 49
    in opening statement for
        prosecution 36
    visited by prison psychiatrist 40
    in evidence on forced labour 46
    testimony of Franz Blaha 62
    evidence against on forced labour
        65
    in evidence on concentration
        camps 71
    gives testimony 131–3
    in Robert Jackson's closing
        statement 158
    final statement of 176
    sentenced to death 178
Scanzoni, Gustav von 25
Schacht, Hjalmar 20, 48, *120*
    defence counsel for 27
    during prosecution opening 31
    reaction to film of concentration
        camp 39
    evidence against 58
    gives testimony 118–22
    in Robert Jackson's closing
        statement 157, 160
    final statement of 176
    acquitted 180
Schellenberg, Walter 167–8

Schilling, Klaus 59
Schirach, Baldur von 20, 49
    reacts to films on Nazi Plan 44
    on Alfred Rosenberg 56
    gives testimony 128, 130–31
    in Robert Jackson's closing
        statement 158
    final statement of 176
    sentenced to imprisonment 179
Schmalevska, Severina 80
Schuschnigg, Kurt 135–6
SD
    on trial 20, 22
    evidence on by Robert Storey 49
    defence counsel for 167
    found guilty 180
Seidl, Alfred
    as defence counsel for Rudolf
        Hess 97, 98
    questions Hans Frank 113
Servatius, Robert 167
Seyss-Inquart, Arthur 20, *135*
    during prosecution opening 31
    gives testimony 135–8
    in Robert Jackson's closing
        statement 158
    final statement of 177
    sentenced to death 178
Shawcross, Hartley
    on prosecution team 25
    opening statement on waging
        aggressive war 44–5
    closing statement of 161–5
Shirer, William 32
Siemers, Walter 38
Sievers, Wolfram 168
simultaneous translation 28–9
Smirnov, Len N. 80
Soviet Union
    damage from war 73–4
    evidence on invasion plans 74–5
    treatment of prisoners of war
        75–6
    prosecutor's style 76–7

191

# INDEX

showing of *The Atrocities of the German Fascist Invaders in the USSR* 77
illegal seizures in 77–78
destruction in 78–9, 92
forced labour in 79–80
Speer, Albert 20, *57*, *135*
  during prosecution opening 31
  in opening statement for prosecution 36
  reaction to Churchill's 'Iron Curtain' speech 84
  gives testimony 140–43
  in Robert Jackson's closing statement 158
  final statement of 177
  sentenced to imprisonment 179
SS
  on trial 20
  evidence on by Warren Farr 49
  affidavit by Hermann Gräbe 49–51
  defence counsel for 169–70
  found guilty 181
Stahmer, Otto
  becomes Göring's defence counsel 26
  and Erwin Lahousen's evidence 41
  calls Karl Bodenschatz 85
  calls Birger Dahlerus 89
  questions Göring 91
  and Katyn Forest massacre 150
Stalin, Joseph
  signs 'Statement on Atrocities' 12
  and United Nations War Crimes Commission 12
  at Tehran Conference 13, *13*, 14
*Stars and Stripes* 42
'Statement on Atrocities' 12
Steinbauer, Gustav 135–6, 152
Stimson, Henry 14

Stoop, Jürgen 36
Storey, Robert
  presents evidence at prosecution opening 37–8
  presents evidence on Nazi leadership 48–9
Streicher, Julius 19, 49, *135*
  during prosecution opening 31
  in opening statement for prosecution 34
  reaction to film of concentration camp 39
  evidence against 58
  gives testimony 115–17
  in Robert Jackson's closing statement 157, 160
  final statement of 175
  sentenced to death 178
Sutzkever, Abraham 80
Taylor, Telford 54–5
Tehran Conference 13–14
*Times, The* 72, 95, 102
Tojo, General 182
Truman, Harry S. 15, 182
United Nations War Crimes Commission 10
Vabres, Henri Donnedieu de 24, 25
Vaillant-Couturier, Marie-Claude 69–71
Vernik, Jacob 82–3
Versailles Treaty 9, 10
Volchkov, A.F. 23, 24, 25
Waffen-SS 169–70
Wallis, Frank 38
Webb, Sir William 182
West, Rebecca 29, 153, 164
Westhoff, Adolf 107
Wielen, Max 107
Wilhelm II, Kaiser 9
Winwood, T.C.M. 27
Wisliceny, Dieter 53–4